SONY

Ajay Sethi is a Delhi-based writer and senior advertising professional. His books include *The Making of the Greatest: Bill Gates* and *The Making of the Greatest: Microsoft*. He has also written numerous magazine articles and devised several advertising and product promotion campaigns. An MA in English Literature from Delhi University, his interests range from politics and history to philosophy and religion.

Also by the author:

The Making of the Greatest: Bill Gates
The Making of the Greatest: Microsoft

THE MAKING OF THE GREATEST
SONY

Ajay Sethi

RUPA

Published by
Rupa Publications India Pvt. Ltd 2021
7/16, Ansari Road, Daryaganj
New Delhi 110002

Sales Centres:
Allahabad Bengaluru Chennai
Hyderabad Jaipur Kathmandu
Kolkata Mumbai

ISBN: 978-93-90918-37-9

First impression 2021

10 9 8 7 6 5 4 3 2 1

The moral right of the author has been asserted.

Printed at Thomson Press India Ltd, Faridabad

CONTENTS

PREFACE

Before the opening up of China in the 1980s, Japan was the second largest economy in the world, after the US. Having slipped to the third position with a GDP of $4.9 trillion as of 2020, it remains one of the formidable economic powers in the world, with businesses straddling all seven continents. In a world comprising about 200 countries (including 193 UN members), anyone can be ahead or behind in the number game. But what makes Japan's achievement special is first, its size and population and second, the fact that it was able to achieve this position against heavy odds, having been beaten and bombed in the Second World War (WWII).

Its special position is surely unique and calls for a deeper analysis of how it was able to reach this standing and what factors helped it in this regard.

Since the subject of this book—Sony Corporation—is one of its major companies, it would be helpful to first look at the background of the country, its history and culture, as no entity exists in isolation and its essential grain, its business philosophy and ethics, are part of its background. In this context, we would also like to understand Japan's geographical and physical position vis-à-vis the rest of the world and see how all those elements combined with other factors to help the country emerge as a major economic power in the post-WWII period—for that would also explain to a considerable extent, the secret of Sony's growth and success.

A NEW WORLD ORDER IN
THE MAKING

To understand Japan's progress, let's analyse how the world evolved after AD 1500, when it had started to move towards a new world order. The discovery of America and the sea route to India were major steps in integrating the world like never before and spurring global trade to an unprecedented level. The dissemination of information and knowledge aided by the printing technology had begun to create new awareness and awakening about the world, and different sections and interest groups had begun to claim their rightful place in the new scheme of things. The world was poised for a major transformation.

There was churning at every level — social, political and economic. Old empires had started to dissolve gradually—Ottoman, Russian, German, Austro-Hungarian, British—and new nation states had begun to appear. Religion was taking a back seat and individualism was on the fore. New ethnic, linguistic and religious entities had begun to assert themselves to claim their place in the new order of things. Fresh political and social alignments had become the order of the day. Concepts like democracy, nationalism, welfare state, etc. had begun to fire the imagination of people. All these issues had to be resolved as per the aspirations of people and specific groups.

So, by the time the world entered the twentieth century, such issues had acquired a certain urgency and the conflicts needed to be resolved to the satisfaction of the warring parties. According to some historians, the period from the First World War (1914–18) to the Second World War (1939–45), was actually a drawn-out civil war, which sought to settle the festering issues. In time, all the old colonies were freed and new nation states appeared on the world map. On the economic front, against the backdrop of these upheavals, a variety of changes took place. As a result, post-1950, while a large part of the world closed itself under the socialist economy, some others opted for free enterprise and mixed economy, yet many former colonies in Asia and Africa continued to struggle to find their bearings in the new scheme of things.

The US wanted to stem the spread of communism and wished to have as many allies as possible. Consequent to this, a comprehensive economic revival plan for Japan was put into effect. During the period 1946–52, the US invested $2.2 billion towards Japan's reconstruction effort. Following the Potsdam Declaration, under the supervision of General Douglas MacArthur, Supreme Commander for the Allied Powers (SCAP), a host of measures were enforced. These included: eliminating Japanese non-defensive armed forces, thereby curbing their right to wage war; introducing land reforms aimed at reducing the power of rich landlords and benefitting the tenant farmers; breaking up large businesses (*Zaibatsu*) in favour of free-market capitalist economy; drafting a new Constitution to downgrade the emperor's status and placing more powers in the parliamentary system; and promoting more rights and privileges for women.

As a result of these measures, the Japanese economy had started to get on its feet. But what proved to be a shot in the arm during this time was the Korean War that commenced in 1950. Japan became the virtual 'supply depot' for the UN forces and got its factories running. 'Korea came along and saved us,' remarked one occupation official. The US formally handed over the power back to the Japanese in 1952, and the Japanese economy started taking off in the subsequent years.

While it is true that the involvement of the US around this time did help Japan get back on its feet, no amount of support or 'stimulus package' can help a country achieve the success that Japan did, let alone claim the 'economic miracle' that's often been attributed to it. In fact, there is much in its previous centuries that led to this. We need to examine all those factors in order to understand Japan's progress over time.

EVOLUTION OF JAPAN AND ITS PEOPLE

History has shown us that geography has always played an important role in a country's destiny. We know that the Indus Valley Civilization couldn't sustain itself because of the climactic changes that led to drier conditions and paucity of water, forcing its population to migrate. Similarly, the hostile and rugged conditions of the Arab world, with its tribal culture, forced people to have a different outlook on life. Similarly, when we look at Japan, we find that its location has had a lot to do with the way its people, their belief systems and thoughts, evolved over the centuries.

Japan is an archipelago of 6,852 islands, part of the 'Pacific Ring of Fire' and very hilly, with 110 active volcanoes. Its tallest mountain, Mt Fuji, stands at 12,389 ft. A mountainous country, with 68.46 per cent of it forested, it leaves very little land for agricultural, industrial or residential activities. There is archeological evidence to suggest that the area had been inhabited as early as 30,000 BC. However, as with most of the other regions of the world, it was only in the first millennium BC, with the onset of the Iron Age that the region started showing signs of growth and progress.

While on one hand, an island-existence affords freedom and independence, on the other, it also raises concerns about security and protection. To protect themselves, people engage in all kinds of defence mechanisms. While the weak succumb to external aggression, the more self-respecting and motivated ones develop different defence systems to protect themselves. Such was the case of the Japanese people. They developed a fierce sense of self-identity that has manifested itself in all its actions and reactions over the ages. Thus, despite being beaten and bombed in WWII, it was able to rise from the ashes and become a major economic power within a short span of time. The character and the spirit that led to this have their roots in their earlier evolution.

Military and Martial Tradition

Owing to its geographical and physical conditions, Japan was able to develop strong maritime, military and martial traditions over the ages. According to historical sources, Japan had diplomatic and cultural exchanges with Korea from the third century onwards and militarily supported the campaign seeking Baekje restoration in 663 CE against the combined aggression of the Silla regime of Korea and the Chinese Tang dynasty.

However, Japan being an archipelago, had much internal conflict also among its own feudal lords and clans controlling different regions. One major arms engagement documented talks of the five-year Genpei War (1180–85) between the Minamoto and Taira clans. During this war, in the decisive naval battle of Dan-no-Ura, the legendary warrior Minamoto no Yoshitsune was able to secure a victory that made the Minamoto clan the de facto rulers of Japan. The weapons of war used during several of these confrontations were bows and arrows, which later gave way to swords.

Japan's engagement with the Mongol armies, led by Kublai Khan in 1274 and 1281, again highlights its maritime and military capabilities. In these conflicts, the

Japanese were up against much larger armies equipped with far superior weaponry. Despite these handicaps, the Japanese were able to hold their own in Kyushu in the 1281 conflict, until most of the Mongol ships were destroyed by a typhoon, hailed as 'divine wind' (*kamikaze*) by the Japanese people. Groups of samurais transported on small coastal boats are recorded to have taken over, damaged and burned many Mongol ships.

However, it was only after the sixteenth century, when different countries had started to come closer due to European seafaring, that serious efforts were made to build a world-class Japanese navy. Proactive steps in this direction included: sending Japanese naval students to the Netherlands in 1862 for maritime training, indigenously building a 140-ton steam-powered gun-boat Chiyodagata in 1863, acquiring the first ocean-going ironclad warship *Kōtetsu* from the US in 1869, developing cruisers with 12.6-inch Canet guns with French help, and adopting advanced technologies such as torpedoes, torpedo boats and mines, again with French assistance. As a result of such consistent efforts, the Japanese were able to build a strong navy, and boasted of the third-largest navy in the world by 1920.

An island nation naturally has to lay stress on a

strong navy, but the ground forces are also indispensable. Starting from the Meiji Era (1868–1912), which heralded the modern times of Japan, the country undertook major steps to build a strong, modern army too. Like most political organizations in the rest of the world around the time, Japan too had been divided into small and big feudatories, controlled by *Daimyos* (*dai*, meaning large and *myo*, short for *myoden*, meaning 'private land'), who in turn were answerable to *Shogun*, the military dictators who were virtually the de facto rulers and were nominally appointed by the emperor. The office of *Shogun* was normally hereditary, though some variations happened over time. The samurai, literally meaning 'to wait upon', were the traditional warrior class that formed the private armies of *Daimyos,* and were the main arms of defence and offence depending upon the situation.

In due course, the whole military-political situation began to change as the country moved towards modernization of the army during the Meiji era. One of the most important legislations brought around this time was the conscription law of 1873 that established military service for all Japanese males above the age of 20 for a duration of three years, with four years in reserve. As the armed forces were mainly the domain of the samurais, this disturbance of the status quo signified a major upheaval for the country. In January 1877, a major revolt led by a prominent samurai Saigō Takamori plunged the country into a civil war. It lasted for about nine months, ending in September, with a decisive victory for the imperial forces, with the rebellious leader Takamori committing *seppuku* (hara-kiri).

Once the dust settled on this conflict, the country was well on its way to be equipped with a well-organized, modern army. Duke Yamagata Aritomo, who was born in a samurai family in Hagi, has been called the main architect of the modern Japanese army. Under his supervision, the Officer Training Institute for Imperial Japanese Army, Kyoto, was renamed the Imperial Japanese Army Academy and relocated to Ichigaya, Tokyo. In 1874, Japan became the first non-European country to modernize its military equipment and systems.

In the beginning, it imported Western arms and weapons, and subsequently, started their domestic manufacture. Following such steps, Japan emerged as an important Asian power in the early twentieth century. Its victory over China in the Sino-Japanese War (1894–95) and Russia in the Russo-Japanese War (1904–05) gave it certain dominance and influence in the region. Within a few decades, it was able to establish a large empire comprising colonies in Manchuria, China, Indonesia, the Philippines, Malaysia, Papua New Guinea, Indochina, Myanmar and many Pacific islands. By 1937, it had one-sixth the industrial capacity of the US. So by the time WWII commenced, it was a powerful nation almost at a par with European countries like Germany, France and the UK.

Culture, Education and Economic Progress

A society moves on the basis of ideas. Intellectual development forms the bedrock of all growth and progress. Given Japan's geographical position, its people were essentially influenced by three streams of thought that have guided their thoughts and behaviour pattern through the ages till the modern times.

Shinto, an indigenous mythological system believes in *Kami*, the supernatural spirits that control the elements and consequently people's destiny. Depending on circumstances, *Kami* assume a positive or negative character. For instance, air, though a life-giving source, can also be extremely destructive in the form of a storm. Or water, a basic life requirement, can play havoc with people's lives during a flood or a tsunami.

Confucianism, although not an organized religion, also has had a major influence on the Japanese people. It came into Japan from Korea in 285 CE and intermingled with other streams of thought. In essence, the belief system lays stress on morality and individual perfection, pursuit of harmony and order in the family, and peace and prosperity in the polity. The prevalence of these teachings influenced Japan's polity, especially during the period of powerful regent Shotoku Taishi, who furthered the cause of a unified rule, reducing the powers of the feudal lords.

Taishi also promoted the teachings of Buddhism that came into Japan in the sixth century CE through Buddhist monks from China. With its eight-fold path to salvation (*nirvana*) — Right View, Right Intention, Right Speech, Right Action, Right Livelihood, Right Effort, Right Mindfulness and Right Concentration — the belief system seeks to release the individual from the cycle of birth and death, and thus suffering. As of 2017, around 70 per cent of the Japanese population participated in

Shinto practices and more than 69 per cent believed in Buddhism, indicating that most Japanese people practise both the religions. About 60 per cent of the population is believed to have a Butsudan (Buddhist shrine) in their homes, while Shinto is known to have about 80,000 shrines across the country.[1]

Religious beliefs apart, as Japanese interaction with the West increased after the sixteenth century, the leaders began to realize that Western ideas and technology were the way forward to put the country on the fast track of technological advancement and industrial progress. During the Meiji era, a concerted effort was launched to increase interface with the West. 'Knowledge shall be sought throughout the world so as to strengthen the foundation of Japanese rule,' was the mantra of the new generation, and part of the Charter Oath or Imperial Oath of Five Articles of 1868, taken by Japanese students. Around this time, thousands of Japanese students were sent to the US and Europe to import the latest technological and industrial ideas. Over 3,000 Western experts were employed in Japan to teach modern sciences, mathematics, technology and foreign languages to students.

As part of the state-led industrialization policy, the

Iwakura Mission went to Europe to explore ways and means to make Japan a modern nation. The Bank of Japan was founded in 1882. Modern steel and textile factories came up all over the county. In 1913, Japan was the fourth-largest yarn exporter in the world, with an export of 672 million pounds every year. The first railway between Tokyo and Yokohama was inaugurated in 1872. Aggressive entrepreneurs were taking advantages of the new policies and taking the country forward. Japan being a resource-scarce country, initiated a comprehensive mercantile policy whereby raw material was imported and finished goods exported.

As a result of this forward movement, a host of companies got established, which followed their own internal dynamic process and began to take advantage of the new industrial and economic ideas elsewhere in the world. Toshiba Corporation was originally founded in 1875 as Tanaka Seisakusho and was the first company to manufacture telegraph equipment in Japan. Kawasaki Heavy Industries Ltd was founded in 1896 and has been engaged in the manufacture of motorcycles, heavy equipment, aerospace and defence equipment and ships. Hitachi Ltd was established in 1910 and its first product was Japan's first 4-Kw induction motor to be used in copper mining.

The present Mitsubishi group has descended from the Mitsubishi *zaibatsu* that was originally established as a shipping company in 1870 and was disbanded in 1947 during the occupation of Japan. Later during the Korean War, after 1952, the ban was lifted and its former constituents formed tie-ups with one another and were allowed to use the Mitsubishi brand name. Panasonic Corporation was originally founded as Matsushita Electric Industrial Co. Ltd in 1918 and was among Japan's first major electronics companies. Nikon Corporation was established in 1917 to produce cameras, lenses and imaging-related products. Following in its footsteps, Precision Optical Instruments Laboratory began operations in 1937. It was later renamed Canon Camera Co. Inc. in 1947, and shortened to Canon Inc. in 1969.

Among the automotive companies, while Toyota started as a division of Toyoda Automatic Loom Works in 1933, it was later established as an independent entity, Toyota Motor Company in 1937. Suzuki Motor Corporation has its origins in Suzuki Loom Works, set up in a small village of Hamamatsu, in 1909. In

1954, it found success in motorcycle manufacturing and changed its name to Suzuki Motor Co. Ltd. Automotive giant Nissan Motor Co. Ltd has its roots in Kaishinsha Motor Car Works, which was established in 1911 and produced Japan's first car, DAT, in 1914. The company, renamed DAT Motorcar Co. in 1925, became a subsidiary of the Nissan Group in 1933 and was finally called Nissan Motor Co. Ltd. The Honda Motor Co. Ltd was incorporated in 1949, after liquidation of its earlier company Honda Technical Research Institute, and by 1964, had become the largest motorcycle manufacturer in the world.

It goes without saying that large-scale industrial and economic activity would not be possible without first providing for qualified and trained manpower. Alive to this fact, the administration had been engaged in setting up institutes of high learning throughout the nation, beginning from the late eighteenth century. University of Tokyo was established in 1877 and Tohoku University in Sendai was established as Tohoku Imperial University in 1907, which has roots in a medical school set up in 1736. Kyoto University was founded in 1897 and Nagoya University in 1871 as a medical school that later became Imperial University in 1939. Kyoto

Institute of Technology, Tokyo Metropolitan University and Chiba University were established in 1949, Osaka University in 1937, Kyushu University in Fukuoka in 1903 and Hokkaido University was founded in 1876, and chartered in 1918. These are among the country's top universities.

SONY—OPENING NEW VISTAS IN ELECTRONICS

I t is clear from the preceding chapters that by the middle of the twentieth century, Japan was an industrially advanced, well-developed, evolved and mature society—and given its inherent strengths, was fully capable of taking care of itself and rebuilding the nation after the debacle of WWII.

In the post-war situation, a large number of self-respecting and proud Japanese people had begun to consider it their duty to participate in the task of nation-rebuilding. The nation was their identity. One such individual was Masaru Ibuka, the co-founder of Sony, who came to perceive his role in the societal mission as one 'to reconstruct Japan and elevate the nation's culture through dynamic technological and manufacturing activities'. The emphasis was 'to apply highly advanced technologies' developed during the war to applications for the 'common households', as expounded in his *Founding Prospectus* released at the company's inauguration on 7 May 1946.[2]

Ibuka states in the *Founding Prospectus* that the company would carefully avoid any 'formal demarcation between electronics and mechanics, and shall create unique products uniting the two fields'. He didn't want to limit the company to just one item or area of activity, but to continuously engage in using technology for the benefit of the common people. The focus was on 'common households', elevating their culture and enriching their experiences—so whether it was a tape recorder, a transistor radio or a TV, computer games or entertainment channels, the target audience was to be the common household. Sony was not to be a product-specific company (like Mercedes-Benz, Boeing or Toyota) but one with a variety of offerings for common households—not hardware but 'heart-ware' for everyday life.

And thus, began Sony's journey, following these guiding principles in letter and spirit. It continued to move on, forever adapting new technologies as they appeared on the world-scene, often making its own improvisations and modifications, and even creating unique products, unheard of or unseen before — which surprised the world. Sony's saga of trials and tribulations, of struggles and triumphs, makes for a fascinating read. In the following chapters, we wish to trace its history, in different phases of development, and see how, from modest beginnings, it has continued to progress from one milestone to another, to emerge as one of the biggest conglomerates in the world.

Making Waves with Tape Recorder and Transistors

From a rice cooker that didn't take off to tape recorders, transistor radios, TVs, videos and a variety of other products that have become part of millions of households all over the world! Sony has indeed come a long way from its fledgling beginnings in post-World War Japan, when it began as a small radio repair shop in 1945 in Tokyo, to the present position of pre-eminence.

Sony's story can be traced to the late 1930s when Ibuka, as representative of his company, Japan Measuring Instruments, had been assisting the Japanese army during the war to design heat-seeking missiles (code-named 'Marque'). After the war, he left both the company and the Japanese army, and set up a small radio repairing unit in September 1945, on the third floor of bombed-out Shirokiya Departmental Store (later Tokyu Department Store, closed in 1999) in Nihonbashi, Tokyo, with a handful of associates. It was called Tokyo Tsushin Kenkyujo (Totsuken), or Tokyo Telecommunications Research Institute.

It was a narrow, bleak room with a switch board and no windows. The financial position of the company was rather precarious as the expenses were being met from Ibuka's dwindling savings. Yet, there was hope in the fact that their services were in demand as a lot of people had war-damaged radios or ones in which the short-wave unit had been disconnected by the military to prevent them from tuning into enemy propaganda. In the pre-TV days, the radio was people's only connection with the outside world. They were hungry for post-war news and eager to learn of the new developments and changes being brought about in their country.

Ibuka's factory repaired all such radios and also made short-wave converters or adapters that could easily modify medium-wave radios into all-wave receiving devices. As Ibuka's unit was able to provide fast and efficient service and make old radios functional again, its clientele started growing. Its popularity caught people's eyes, and on 6 October 1945, journalist Ryuzo Kaji wrote a feature about Ibuka's set-up in the popular column 'Blue Pencil' in *Asahi Shimbun*, Japan's second-largest newspaper at the time. 'We have welcome news that even the most ordinary radio sets can be modified to receive short-wave broadcast with a simple adjustment,' he wrote. 'When in the near future, private broadcasting is licensed again... Mr Ibuka assures us that the rebuilt sets or those fitted with his adapter will have no trouble picking up the new signals.'[3]

Akio Morita, who had been recruited as a sub-lieutenant in the Japanese navy, had worked in the Japanese Imperial Army's Wartime Research Committee, where he had made the acquaintance of Ibuka and the two had developed a certain rapport. On reading the article, he decided to renew the relationship, and subsequently came to Tokyo to see him. With signs of the war ending, Morita had already decided to quit his job in the navy and make a career for himself in the sciences — as a physicist or a teacher of physics. When an opportunity presented him with his former teacher,

Gakujun Hattori, asking him to join as a lecturer at Tokyo Institute of Technology, he was keen to accept it. But when he saw the *Asahi Shimbun* article about Ibuka, he began to weigh his options. For six months, he worked as a teacher with Hattori, while giving his spare time to Ibuka's set-up. Later when he got permission from his father to join Ibuka's business, he knew that the die had been cast.

Morita's family had been in the sake, miso and soy sauce business since 1665, and had had the means to make significant business investments. As Morita saw a future for himself in this venture, his family made an investment in it, and in time, became a major shareholder of the company. The new company, called Tokyo Tsushin Kogyo Kabushiki Kaisha (Tokyo Telecommunications Engineering Corporation), or Totsuko, in short, was capitalized at 1,90,000 yen[4], and was formally inaugurated on 7 May 1946 with over 20 staff members in attendance. This new development also came as a much-needed relief for Ibuka as it somewhat helped the company to financially stabilize their operation in the long run. Ibuka's father-in-law, Tamon Maeda, a former diplomat and politician, was an influential person with extensive contacts in the government and the industry, and played a significant role in giving the company a push.

From this point, the staff just needed to put their heads down, focus on their goals and give their best towards making a success of their venture. In the initial years, the unit kept on developing and moving from one product to another—some did well while others didn't. Electric rice cookers, megaphones, electrically-heated cushions for the winter months, record (player) pickups and military-use wireless equipment converted into relay receivers for broadcasting supplications were some of the items which were produced around this time. But Ibuka and Morita were keen to develop something major—something new and revolutionary that would have a mass appeal and take the company forward.

Tape Recorder

Foresighted as he was, Ibuka thought that since radios were being manufactured by many companies, they would give it a pass, and pick something new and different—a product that would fire the people's imagination. Given their regular interaction with the

Occupation Forces, the idea of developing an audio tape recorder germinated in his mind. Sound recorders that used magnetic wire and magnetic tape as the recording medium had been around since the invention of the magnetic wire recorder by Danish engineer Valdemar Poulsen (1869–1942) in 1899, and subsequently of magnetic tape for recording by German engineer Fritz Pfleumer (1881–1945) in 1928.

Modern magnetic tape recorders were the outcome of the efforts of American companies such as Brush Development Company and its licensee, Ampex, and Minnesota Mining and Manufacturing Company (3M). Since the wire recorder had been used by the Japanese military during the war, Ibuka thought of improvising on the machine that could serve as a useful item for the general public. The product struck Ibuka as a suitable potential candidate for the manufacturing push they had been looking for. Though, soon after they had begun work on the wire recorder, they decided to give up on it and switch gears. This switch had been prompted by a visit to the Occupation Forces headquarters at the NHK (Japan's public broadcaster) building, where Ibuka came across a tape recorder, and was astonished by its sound quality, which was much superior to that of the wire recorder. 'This is it,' he had said. 'This is what we ought to produce for the consumer market. It has great potential. Let's do it with tape.'

In 1946, Brush Development Company had come out with the first modern consumer tape recorder, and subsequently, 3M had been successful in replacing the paper backing (base material of the tape) with improved-quality cellulose acetate (or polyester). For a new, struggling Japanese company like Totsuko, given the conditions prevalent at the time, the development of a marketable, acceptable product was going to be a rough road.

Nevertheless, by picking up any bits of information or technical details about the product from whatever sources possible, they began their work. It was a road riddled with all kinds of pebbles, barriers and hurdles. From producing the magnetic powder (ferric oxide) from oxalic ferrite using rudimentary methods like processing it in a frying pan, achieving the desired fineness of the magnetic powder, adding clear shellac, coating the tape with the hair of the Tanuki (Japan's beloved raccoon dog) and finding the right motor and rubber—it was a long process of evolution, trial and error in the development of the magnetic powder, base tape material, coating and the mechanism of the system. Gradually, their efforts began to bear fruit.

In the beginning of 1950, the technical team led by Nobutoshi Kihara was able to present two prototypes of the tape recorder: G-type aimed at the institutions (government) with one-hour playback time and A-type for the general consumer with half-hour playback duration. The G-type was taken into production first. As it was targeted towards the government and institutions, it could be used for recording speeches, conversations, etc. Yet, because of its bulk and weight, marketing it was proving to be difficult. Since a product can't be commercially successful without volume production, Ibuka decided to work on it again. 'The G-type tape recorder is too bulky,' he said.' 'If we make a more portable tape recorder, it cannot fail to sell.'

Following this, the company decided to concentrate its efforts on developing a sleeker, smarter version of the machine with improved playback sound that incorporated many features of the A-type in the new model. With further R&D, the technical team was able to bring down the weight of the recorder from the earlier bulky size to 13 kg, less than one-third of the original weight. The machine, rechristened the H-type (home), was introduced in March 1951 and was ready to be marketed.

Despite having overcome the first hurdles, marketing the H-type was a whole new ball game. Why would people buy an expensive electronic item unless they knew what to do with it? For the ordinary household, it could be, at the most, an audio replica of a photograph—preserving memories of family members in their voice recording or their child's recitation of a nursery rhyme learnt at school. To that end, it was an expensive proposition for a householder and thus, difficult to sell during those early days. When it came to the institutional buyers, there was a need to prove its usefulness to them to secure bulk orders—so necessary to make production commercially viable.

The company got to work on this. Some of the initiatives undertaken by the company around this time included establishing a dedicated Society for Sound Recording in Education on the theme of 'How an Audio Visual Education Should Be Offered', hosting special demonstrations at schools wherein educational programmes from NHK were edited and played along 16-mm films, helping the Ministry of Education and NHK organize conventions with teachers all over Japan to demonstrate the usefulness of the tape recorder in education promotion and lending the machines to them. Gradually, these efforts began to pay off, and the school market became one of the major captive clients and the largest buyer of the H-type tape recorder. Besides this, radio stations, music and dance academies, companies (for dictation) and high net-worth individuals who bought the H-type for its novelty-appeal, came to be part of their customer profile and target audience.

As the company engineers got a better grip on the technology, they were able to come out with sleeker, lighter and cheaper models, more in the nature of what the general consumer desired. Model-P (portable) proved to be its cash cow, selling over 3,000 units in just seven months. And the next model, Model-M (movie), which was modelled after a machine manufactured by an American company for paratroopers in the Korean War, fared even better. At about 9 kg, it was lighter and ideal for street interviews that had been coming into vogue those days. It sold even more than the earlier models.

Around this time, a major Japanese company Matsushita Electric Industrial Co. Ltd (later Panasonic) also came out with its own brand of tape recorders. The entry of a competitor was naturally a cause of concern for Totsuko. To their surprise, however, it didn't affect their sales—on the contrary, helped to boost it. Since the idea of a tape recorder was rather new, the introduction of another brand helped to popularize the basic concept of the tape recorder, and in turn, benefitted both the parties. From these experiences and events, Ibuka and Morita also learnt some early lessons in marketing: first, the best market could be found only by developing the market itself—as the company had done with the education market—or in other words, 'dig a trench before you drain water'; and second, a competitor is not always your rival—he could even be your promoter, indirectly.

Transistor

It had been six years since the inception of their company, and with the tape recorder, they had been able to taste their first major success. Apart from being a factor in stabilizing their finances, it had also proved to be a major morale-boosting development.

Perennially on the lookout for new avenues to scale up the company's operation, in March 1952, Ibuka decided to travel to the US to expand his horizons with respect to the international marketing trends. In Japan, although the tape recorder had been a well-accepted product in the school market, Ibuka wanted to expand this market and have a first-hand experience of American marketing, and see for himself how it was proving to be a useful item for the American consumers. He also planned to personally gain knowledge of American manufacturing by visiting some facilities.

Sometimes, a chance event in life can prove to be a turning point. This is what happened with Ibuka in New York. An old acquaintance came to see him in the hotel he was staying at and told him that Western Electric, the parent company of Bell Laboratories and which held the patent for the transistor, had decided to release the transistor licence to interested parties. When the transistor was invented in 1947, Ibuka was shown an article to this effect, but at that time, he had dismissed it with the words, 'No, I don't think a thing like this will ever do.'

The transistor[5], which was a replacement for vacuum tubes used in electrical appliances, later leading up to the Integrated Circuit (IC) and then the microprocessor, was set to change the entire ecosystem of the industrial world in the future. It was invented in December 1947 by Dr W.B. Shockley, Dr John Bardeen and Dr W. Brattain while researching at the Bell Laboratories. However, at this stage, people were unable to figure out what exactly to do with it and what applications it could be used for.

The situation was different compared to earlier times, and he began to think about how he could use the transistor. With tape recorder manufacturing in full swing, his company, with newly employed staff had become top-heavy, and he thought the introduction of a new concept could channel his personnel's energies well. Perhaps in a different situation, he might have thought otherwise. He decided to go for it, with an aim to produce transistor radios with it. Though, due to some scheduling issues, he was unable to meet the Western Electric people. He left the US with some regret, and a diode (a semiconductor) and a vinyl tablecloth as souvenirs, as these products were not available in Japan.

The eight years following 1952 would prove to be extremely crucial and challenging for the company. As Ibuka had made up his mind, the company decided to go ahead with its new project of the transistor radio.

In pursuance of this, Morita travelled to the US, and in August 1953 was able to sign the licence agreement with Western Electric. This set the ball rolling. The next steps included dealing with the Ministry of International Trade and Industry (MITI), winning over the credit division of the Mitsui Bank, setting up a dedicated transistor-manufacturing facility at Sendai (in the Miyagi district, 370 km from Tokyo and among paddy fields) and recruiting new personnel, including 'transistor girls' to operationalize the unit.

There was one disconcerting point though. As the licence agreement with Western Electric didn't cover technology, the Totsuko engineers didn't have much to go by. Their bible at the time was *Transistor Technology*, a compilation made by the Western Electric engineers, which Morita had brought from the US. It could serve as a starting point. They had no other research material, let alone the technical know-how. Giving up was not an option. Western Electric would not share the technical specifications but were willing to show the Japanese around their manufacturing plants.

So, in January 1954, Kazuo Iwama, the general manager of the project, went to the US to study the manufacturing processes and was later joined by Ibuka.

Iwama spent about four months in the US, visiting the transistor plants, talking to Western Electric engineers, taking detailed notes and gathering as much information as possible on transistor technology. When he would return to his hotel room in the evening, he would draw illustrations from memory and make exhaustive reports to send back home for his people to work on. Although not very proficient in English, he was sending home the material in a mix of two languages. Given the constraints, the manufacturing of radio transistors was to be a purely indigenous effort, as there was no template to go by as yet. Even according to the Western Electric engineers, given the transistor's low frequency output, it could perhaps best be used for making hearing aids only. The idea of hearing aids had been dismissed outright by Ibuka, as he knew the Japanese considered it to be an embarrassing contraption, and so didn't like to use one. We must understand that any invention is essentially a basic idea—people build on it depending on their needs and imagination. What humanity has done with the wheel doesn't call for an explanation today.

Thus, the Totsuko engineers were determined to make transistor radios and plodded on, coming up with innovative techniques, materials and out-of-the-box solutions. In the process, they were even able to achieve a major breakthrough which was later termed as 'The Esaki Diode'. This semiconductor was produced by a young Totsuko engineer, Dr Leo Esaki, who later joined IBM and shared the Nobel Prize for Physics in 1973 along with Ivar Giaever and Brian David Josephson for his work in electron tunneling in semiconductor materials.

In time, the engineers' efforts began to pay off and they were able to come out with the prototype of their first transistor radio, TR-52, in October 1954. Meanwhile, in December 1954, they came to know that an American company called Regency had announced its transistor radio Model TR-1, and had become the first company in the world to produce a transistor radio. Although the Totsuko people were a little disappointed initially, they felt reassured by the fact that the Regency Radio had used the transistors manufactured by Texas Instruments, while their's was an all-indigenous effort. Further, it was a superior product that used five-junction transistors, against the four of Regency, for better sound quality.

With some improvements on the TR-52 prototype

the TR-55 model was released in August 1955. It had had the distinction of being Japan's first transistor radio. With this, Totsuko also became the first company to manufacture its own transistors and other components to produce the radio. The ad of the first catalog stated: 'The days of radios with cords are over. Why not make the change in your home? Your transistor radio can accompany you wherever you go.'

Many other models were released over the following years, but two stand out. The TR-63 released at the beginning of 1957 was the world's smallest transistor radio (or the 'pocket radio'), and the first to be exported at a price tag of $39.95. Its demand was so high that regular consignments couldn't cope with it and a special JAL plane had to be chartered to satisfy the customers. It is estimated that by the mid-1960s, the model had sold about seven million units all over the world. To reinforce its 'pocket-size' image, the company even got the uniforms of the personnel altered—with larger front pockets on the shirts to accommodate the radio. The next one, TR-610, still smaller and lighter than TR-63, beat all expectations. Introduced in June the same year, with an innovative design and superior sound, it sold half a million sets worldwide, including in Japan—so much so it even commanded a premium in some markets. In the truest sense, Sony had arrived. Subsequently, the company was able to launch a variety of models to suit different audiences.

TAKING ON THE WORLD

I t was Monday, 1 October 1962. The occasion was the opening of the Sony Showroom on the upscale Fifth Avenue, New York. Among the guest list of over 400 invitees was the Consul General of New York. As the formal inauguration got underway, the Japanese and American guests joined in the celebrations and congratulated one another. Not only for Sony, but for all of Japan, it was quite a historic moment—a matter of pride. For the first time since WWII, the Japanese flag had flown high on the American soil. Sony—and in a way Japan too—had arrived on the world scene!

The period between the early 1960s and the mid-1980s can be termed as one of growth and consolidation for Sony. Their pioneering research efforts in the field of magnetic tape recorder and transistor had earned them recognition and respect all over the world. We could say a foundation had been laid. All they had to do now was to build a skyscraper — which they did! As the demand for their products grew, 'Go global' became the mantra at the company. It was a production necessity too. After all, how much volume could the domestic market absorb? Yet, given their current position, both the promoters knew they had a long way to go.

On his first visit to the US, Ibuka had been rather awestruck by the size of the country, its tall buildings and shining automobiles. He had also felt disturbed by the racial discrimination he had experienced at the Anchorage (Alaska's largest city) airport. Morita too, on his visit in 1953, had felt a little intimidated by America's size and had had doubts if the Western Electric people would entertain an entrepreneur from a small Japanese company. In the Netherlands, however, he had a different experience. He felt more at home there and self-assured while visiting the Philips facility. He thought if a company from such a small country could command global reach, why wouldn't their own company, Totsuko, be able to make its mark. Despite all their apprehensions, the formidable duo did have confidence in their abilities and were determined to get ahead.

At this stage, one major stumbling block for the company was the finances—a critical factor in any expansion and diversification. Large, established companies such as Toshiba, Hitachi, Mitsubishi, etc. operating since the beginning of the century, had tie-ups with specific banks, and thus were comfortably placed in that respect. But Totsuko, being a new company, didn't enjoy much clout with financial institutions, and thus began to have difficulty in raising funds. To overcome this, they were advised to take the direct route of the Stock Exchange to raise money from the market. Having earned some repute in their 10 years of operation, the company was able to list their stock in the over-the-counter market of the Tokyo Stock Exchange on 8 August 1955.

As it had shown moderate appreciation in the initial years, in December 1958, the stock got listed in the first section of the Exchange. The main thrust however came in 1961 when the company was shortlisted by the Ministry of Finance, along with 15 others, to be permitted to issue ADRs (American Depository Receipts) that facilitated stock transaction on the New York Stock Exchange. In the beginning of June 1961, Sony ADR (offering 10 shares in a block) was listed on the New York Exchange and was offered at $17.50. In just an hour, two million shares had been completely sold off. And even those who bought the ADR at $23 were being offered premium.

With different pieces falling into place, the company embarked on a major expansion programme. One of the first major steps in this direction was to set up Sony Corporation of America (SONAM) in 1960 to have direct control of the marketing, after a few unpleasant experiences with the local American distributors. From this point onwards, the process of establishing offices and manufacturing facilities, both domestically and internationally, got underway on a vigorous and sound footing.

The Atsugi transistor plant was set up in 1960 and Sony Research Centre came up in Hodogaya, Yokohama, in 1961. In 1968, Sony Hawaii was founded, and the next year, Sony of Canada Ltd was incorporated. Sony Overseas S.A (SOSA) was established in Zürich, in December 1960, to oversee European operations. New colour TV plants were also set up in the 1970s in Barcelona (Spain) and Stuttgart (Germany). A showroom at the up-market Champs-Élysées (Paris) was opened in September 1971. In 1970, Sony GmbH,

Cologne, and in February 1973, Sony France were founded. On 3 August 1972, a colour TV plant at San Diego, California, and two years later, one in Bridgend in Wales (UK) came up. Subsequently, a speaker plant in Delano, Pennsylvania, in 1974, a video-cassette plant in Dothan, Alabama, in 1977, and an audio-cassette tape plant in Nuevo Laredo, Mexico, in 1979, were established. As the company grew further, it continued to expand its reach and presence in different parts of the world on an ongoing basis.

On the product-development front, the success of the tape recorder and transistor radio had boosted the company's confidence and morale. Now they were looking towards new frontiers. 'The days of radio are over. The future lies in television.' This was Ibuka's clear message to his people—and as ever, Ibuka wouldn't just follow the beaten track. The immediate goal was to develop a transistorized TV. Around this time, with initiatives being taken by different companies in Europe and the US, TV production had picked up pace, and it had started to be a sought-after household item. It's estimated that while in 1946 only 0.5 per cent of the US households had a TV, by 1954 and 1962, the figure had gone up to 55.7 per cent and 90 per cent, respectively.

In the UK, 15,000 TV households in 1947 had grown to 1.4 million by 1952 and 15.1 million by 1968. As colour technology was in its nascent stage and was somewhat distant, the majority of the TVs sold in Japan were black and white sets.

In this scenario, Sony didn't want to introduce just another such TV in the market. It prided itself for its 'innovation' capabilities, of doing something new and different. Over time, it had begun to gain greater experience and expertise in transistor development and it wished to make use of this strength for its new electronic items. With the focus on producing a transistorized TV, the engineers' experience in radio transistors was not enough—this was a different ball game altogether. Compared to radio, which leaves some room for error since it is audio alone, in the case of TV, imperfections appear bright and clear on the screen. The engineers began their research in 1958 to produce transistors and other components that would help them circumvent this problem and create a new product. After a year of experimentation and trial and error, the team succeeded in developing a small TV which would be called TV8-301, the world's first direct-view portable TV.

When it went on sale in 1960, it was considered a major breakthrough in the world of electronics, and being the first transistorized TV, was talked about in the professional circles. Yet, from the marketing point of view, it was not a big success as it broke down often, and compared to the regular home console set, worked out expensive. Much to the chagrin of the engineering team, it came to earn the nickname of Sony's 'frail little baby'. However, the positive fallout of this was that the invaluable experience gained in its development was to lead the company to a smarter and better product soon.

With every new product, Sony had begun to acquire a certain grip over miniaturization. Upbeat with its successes, the focus of the Sony team was now on a five-inch TV, to be positioned as a 'car TV'. Fortunately for the company, around this time, Bell Labs, the original inventor of the transistor, announced the development of an 'epitaxial transistor'; this was good news for Sony. The engineers felt this transistor was ideally suited for their five-inch TV. They test manufactured silicon epitaxial mesa transistors, which measured up to their expectations.

With the main task achieved, they dealt with other glitches, including testing the prototype at high speeds in a car to see how it would withstand vibrations, the effect on its performance by the intercepting radio waves and noise generated by the car while in motion. Finally, the new TV, christened micro-TV, went on sale on 4 October 1962. On account of its novelty factor and its performance, the product caught people's imagination, and was well accepted in the market. The demand was so high that as shipping took time, on 7 November, the company had to charter a special Pan American plane to deliver the product in the US.

Trinitron—A Star Is Born

The management was obviously happy with the reception of their new transistorized small TVs — but that was not their ultimate goal. These attempts could be seen as a dry run for the 'real thing'. What would bring joy and glory to both Ibuka and Morita would be a full-size (19–20 inch) colour TV that would appeal to the masses. In the early '60s, however, the technology of colour TVs was still in an evolving phase. Most of the colour TVs of this time used cathode-ray tube (CRT) based on the 'shadow mask' system, developed by Radio Corporation of America (RCA). The 'shadow mask' refers to a thin metal sheet with tiny holes punched into it, used just behind the glass screen of the TV. Not only was the price of such TVs high, even the picture quality was not satisfactory as the colours didn't come out bright and alive. Unsurprisingly, few customers went for it and its overall sale percentage against the black-and-white TVs was very low.

Given the general dissatisfaction with the 'shadow mask' system, Ibuka and his team had been looking for a better alternative. One possible option was the Chromatron CRT tube that had been developed by Ernest Lawrence, who was awarded the Nobel Prize for Physics in 1939. It utilized a different technology and promised better and brighter colours. This decision in favour of Chromatron, however, proved quite troublesome in the long run as the engineers began to encounter one problem after the other as the project got underway in 1962. The technology was suitable for some other applications, but for a proper 19-inch colour console, it posed different issues. Technical issues apart, the expensive Chromatron pack, and the high cost of the extra man-hours became a big overhang on the project. Although within two years, in September 1964, the Sony technical team was able to unveil Chromatron

TV and the sales had begun, matters were far from being satisfactory. Besides questions about the TV's performance, the overall production costs were a cause of worry. As the whole project somewhat threatened to derail the company's finances, Ibuka, Morita and the senior management staff began a rethink on the project. 'Are you sure that the shadow mask doesn't deserve reconsideration?' Ibuka asked, raising the issue at a board meeting.

Different options were weighed. Changes such as the use of one combined electronic gun instead of three, experimentation with the phosphor and fluorescent material (used at the back of the glass screen) were some of the options considered. As luck would have it, the breakthrough came during experimentation when one of the team leaders, Ohgoshi, replaced the punched metal sheet (the 'shadow mask') with a metal grille that had vertical stripes photo-etched on a thin metal plate stretched over a frame. This was the 'eureka moment' that would carry their ship home safely and smoothly.

While the shadow mask system used a thin metal plate punched with tiny holes behind the TV screen, the Chromatron technology used woven wires. So, as the electronic beams of the primary colours for TV (red, green and blue) were fired at the screen from the back, the electrons filtering through the tiny holes, or woven wires, would activate the coloured phosphor material etched on the layer behind and behind and produce an all-colour image on the screen. As the grille (suggested by Ohgoshi) allowed a higher percentage of electrons to filter through the barrier, compared to the metal sheet or the shadow mask, it was able to produce 25 per cent brighter images on the screen. The new technology came to be known as the 'Aperture Grille' method, and Sony marketed its new TV under the brand name of Trinitron—derived from trinity of the basic colours, red, green and blue, and electron. The TV was formally launched in October 1968.

Sony's long, hard work on the colour TV had paid off. Trinitron proved to be a big success for the company, known for its innovations and new products, and was a major revenue earner in the long run. With its superior quality and brighter colours, Aperture Grille and three-colour beam in single gun technology, the Trinitron was a winner. Its sales began to soar. Interestingly, in the mid-1970s in the US, the computer revolution had also begun, with the concept of the PC firing people's imagination. Given its better quality, the

Trinitron CRT also became the tube of choice for a host of computer manufacturers.

It's estimated that by June 1994, about 25 years since its launch, over 100 million Trinitron CRTs had been sold — with about half this number being manufactured in just the preceding five years. It was steadily climbing the popularity charts, and the Trinitron also became the first TV receiver to be awarded the prestigious Emmy Award in 1973. On his 84th birthday, Ibuka claimed that Trinitron was the product he was proudest of, and Morita often said, 'The Trinitron is the most important asset after the Sony brand name.'

It was right in another sense too. The success of the Trinitron tube, in a way, helped Sony to turn the corner. Its tremendous sale over the years gave the company the financial muscle to take some bold investment decisions and weather future storms.

VTR, VCR–Betamax and VHS

A forward-looking, well-staffed company generally cannot afford to risk its future on just one or two products. With this shared vision, both Ibuka and Morita had been constantly looking for new avenues of growth. So, along with TV, work had begun on video tape recorders (VTRs) also. After the success of the audio tape recorder, it was the next logical step. In 1956, Ampex Corporation of the US had come out with its first video tape recorder for the broadcasting houses and TV stations. The innovation was of immense use for such networks, and the concept had starting becoming popular. From the 1960s onwards, till the arrival of the digital gadgets, there was much development and competition in this area. The main players in the field included Toshiba, Hitachi, Ampex, JVC and Sony.

Sony's forays into the field became a process of evolution for it, with one product leading to another, until some major successes were achieved. In November 1959, by sharing know-how with Ampex, they were able to produce the world's first transistorized Ampex-style VTR, SV-201, and subsequently PV-100 on their own in September 1962, which was about one-fiftieth the weight of the broadcast-type VTR. Interestingly, it also became the first airborne VTR to be used for in-flight entertainment by American Airlines and Pan American Airways. Sony's next offering in the line was CV-2000, which was a further improvement on the earlier products.

But then, keen businessmen as they were, both Ibuka and Morita knew that volume sales could only be achieved by making a consumer-friendly product for the general household—and as yet their VTRs were far from it. It was not only imperative to reduce the weight and bulk of the machine, but also make it convenient for the common householder to use. By 1975, around 75 per cent of the Japanese households had come to own colour TVs, and the induction of a video recorder would add another dimension to brighten up their lifestyle. Also, with the new technology it had become possible to encase the audio tape in a plastic cassette which had replaced the open reel-to-reel spool system. Now, the same technology, could be applied to encase the video tapes too and make it easier to handle. Keeping all these factors in mind, the Sony team got to work to produce a people's video cassette recorder (VCR), and was able to present the prototype of the U-matic VCR in 1969—named thus as the tape followed a 'U' pattern when loaded.

It was a fine machine, with a good-quality colour picture—yet, given the technology and the production cost involved, it was still an expensive gadget for the common householder. On the other hand, for the broadcasting houses and institutions, it was a welcome product and was received well. The quest was still on for a more convenient and affordable home-use VCR, and in May 1975, Sony engineers were able to come out with the Betamax VCR SL-6300. The cassette was two-thirds the weight of the U-matic with half-an-inch tape width.

As the number of colour TVs in Japanese households had increased substantially, the Betamax was a new entertainment diversion for people. Morita called it 'time-shift.' With Betamax sales rising satisfactorily, Sony was caught off guard in September 1976 when JVC came out with its own version of a VCR with the video home system (VHS) format. It offered two hours of recording and playback time, against one hour of Sony's Betamax. It must be understood that for such devices, a unification of standards and specifications is both in the interests of the consumer and the industry. One year before the launch of the Betamax, Sony representatives had visited JVC and Matsushita, its partners in U-matic, and had disclosed technical information about the Betamax, which they had been developing. The jolt to Sony was that although the VHS format offered more playback time, it was in many ways similar to Betamax. Now, there were two video cassette formats in the market.

This split the industry into two camps, with Toshiba, Sanyo Electric, NEC, Aiwa and Pioneer supporting Sony's Beta, and Matsushita, Hitachi, JVC, Mitsubishi Electric, Sharp and Akai Electric opting for VHS. The famous Beta vs. VHS war ensued. Another point to be noted here is that as the video concept became more popular, with people having the option to view their favourite programmes or films anywhere and everywhere, the entire business came to be heavily video-rental dependent. Video libraries sprang up everywhere. Since a two-hour video was generally enough for a complete film, VHS began to steal a march over Betamax.

Sony's product offered superior picture quality, though it was a little more expensive than the VHS. Several practical advantages weighed in favour of VHS. Moreover, from 1983 onwards, most movie studios began to offer their films on VHS, which again tilted the balance in its favour. Although Sony initially resisted the VHS, realizing the need to adjust to the reality, they started offering both the formats and even offered more options in Betamax. Given its inherent strengths, the Beta wouldn't disappear from the market and the efforts of Sony engineers didn't go waste. Since Betamax released superior picture quality, it was able to hold its own, albeit with a lesser market share in the consumer segment. And with many other advantages, both the U-matic and the Betamax were eventually able to make inroads into the commercial segment and were well-received in broadcasting houses and TV networks. The Betamax video-cassette production was discontinued only on 10 November 2015, after 41 years of continuous production.

With the video concept becoming popular, resistance came from another quarter — the film industry. Universal Pictures Inc. filed a case in court to this effect on the grounds that it directly affected film sales and even encouraged piracy. After a protracted legal battle, that went up to the Supreme Court and lasted for over eight years, the court ruled in favour of Sony, upholding citizens' interests. The lead here was taken by Sony and the entire industry benefitted from the positive outcome of the case.

With a VCR, one could record one's favourite programme or watch the latest movie, but what about personal recordings — of family get-togethers, functions, important meetings, etc. Sony was always a step ahead in anticipating consumers' needs. In July 1980, Sony was able to announce its 'Video Movie', a single unit camera and recorder; in January 1985, a video camcorder; in May 1989, the CCD-TR 55 camcorder, the world's smallest and lightest video recorder weighing just 790 grams. With the onset of the digital age, the designs and technology of electronic items took on a whole new dimension.

In the early 1980s, the digital age was upon the world, and Sony had begun to take baby steps in it. Yet, it signed off the 'tape era' with another innovation and surprise for the world — the 'Walkman'! Many people were apprehensive about its acceptance as it just played sound, and didn't record. Yet, Ibuka's gut feeling told him that it would work. And so it did. Positioned as a lifestyle-statement for the young, up-and-about generation, it became a sensation over time. In 1989, 10 years after the launch of the first model, over 50 million units had been manufactured, a figure that reached 150 million by 1995, with over 300 different models having been produced.

GOING DIGITAL

'll let you work on a replacement for the abacus, but I won't allow you to design a mainframe computer.' That was Ibuka's firm warning to Saburo Uemura of the Research Department, when he found him working on an electronic calculator on the stealth. 'Our products are for the consumer. An electronic calculator just won't sell.' It was the early 1960s and the computer age was yet to arrive. Ibuka had had some reservations about the digital items as he perhaps thought that such efforts would divert the company's attention from the main focus and dissipate energies of the personnel in a different direction. But then, you can't stop the change, 'the idea whose time has come', and have to deal with it when it comes.

In the early 1980s, Sony needed to deal with major challenges on two fronts: adapting to the new digital technologies and restructuring within the organization on account of the founders gradually taking a back seat. The issue of restructuring will be taken up in the next chapter, but we will first analyse Sony's digital forays from the 1980s onwards.

Sony had begun to take tentative steps in the digital arena when Heitaro Nakajima of NHK joined the company in 1971. Having worked on digital audio in his previous assignment, he was keen to use his expertise here too. Nakajima had the full support of Noria Ohga, who was an important voice in the organization and, interestingly, had also been a baritone earlier. The technology Nakajima began working on was called PCM (pulse code modulation) that had been conceptually mooted in 1939, and later had been used for long-distance communication from space by astronauts and other spacemen. Its full potential hadn't been realized till this time.

After working on the project with his team, Nakajima was able to first develop X-12DTC, and later PCM-1 in September 1977 which was designed for home use. However, since it was bulky and had to be used along with a VCR, it proved difficult to market. As efforts in this direction were underway, Sony was able to display its audio disc system along with two other companies in Audio Fair 1977—with Sony's system scoring over the competitors as it recorded digital audio signals compared to the others that used video signals.

Through digital audio technology, audio data is converted into binary digital signals in the form of an array of 'zeroes' and 'ones', and then recorded onto the audio disc, which is metallic, unlike the LP (long playing record) disc, which is made from vinyl plastic. When the disc is played, the digital signals recorded on it are reconverted into electronic signals with a light beam reading them. This technology needed to be perfected to produce digital audio systems of the time.

CD with Philips

Sony's efforts in this regard got a fillip when it had the opportunity to collaborate with Philips, which had made numerous pioneering innovations in electronics. The times were such that a lot of electronics companies had been working on the digital audio technology, and Philips had been looking to replace the conventional vinyl LP with a compact metallic disc. Sony's association with Philips went back to the mid-1960s, when the two had worked together to achieve global standardization in audio compact cassettes. Around this time, Norio Ohga, who was the President of CBS/Sony Records Inc. got a telex message from L.F. Ottens, a Philips executive, requesting a meeting the next time he was in Europe. Ottens wished for Sony's participation in the development of the audio compact disc they had been working on.

Having known Philips for a long time, Ohga was more than willing to go along with them. He got to meet Ottens in June 1978, and felt encouraged by the progress achieved by Philips in this regard. Following exchanges between executives, the two companies agreed to work on the project, and present a prototype at the Digital Audio Disc conference that was to be held in June 1980. The conference comprised 29 companies from around the world who had begun talks to achieve standardization in audio digital disc technology in 1977.

At the Digital Audio Disc conference held in June 1980 in Salzburg, Austria, the prototypes of two other companies besides Sony, Telefunken and JVC, were assessed. In the Sony-Philips system, a smooth layer of plastic covered the audio signals recorded as series of bits along the disc, which was entirely free of grooves. The pickup device could read the audio signals below the protected surface using optical technology, without coming in direct contact with the disc surface. Besides other advantages, this also ensured a longer life for both the system and the disc. On the other hand, Telefunken proposed a mechanical system and JVC an electrostatic system, which suffered a lot of accompanying issues of the conventional technology. At the time, the conference reserved its decision and later in April 1981 announced that it had decided to endorse systems of both Sony-Philips and JVC, barring Telefunken's.

Confident of their superior offering, Sony and Philips continued to further improve upon their system and in August 1982 officially announced the launch of CDP-101. It went on sale in October the same year. With technology that surely had an edge, it proved to be a game changer and shook up the entire industry. New entrants apart, it also disturbed the status quo. What about the companies with huge existing investments in the conventional vinyl LP technology? Even Sony and Philips themselves with their record companies, CBS and Polygram respectively, would need to gradually shift their operations to the new concept at the cost of new investments. Nevertheless, given its clear advantages, the Sony-Philips CD started gaining ground and in time became the de facto industry standard.

CCD—the Electronic Eye

Another major contribution of Sony to the digital world has been its new developments and innovations in respect to CCD (charge-coupled device). This device is basically a light-sensitive IC (integrated circuit) that was invented by Willard Boyle and George E. Smith at Bell Labs in 1969. With its unique design, it had the ability to convert the captured light into digital data, which would be recorded by the camera. (After all, both light and electricity are different forms of energy—and it was like converting one form of energy into another.) Given this unique feature, it would prove instrumental in creating digital imagery, and thus digital cameras and camcorders. On a CCD chip the pixels are neatly aligned together, and as a pixel receives optical signal, it converts it into electric signal and stores it—thus creating a digital image. The natural corollary to this being the greater the number of pixels on a chip, the better the image resolution!

Sony took on the chip when it was still a basic device, and began working on it to produce digital cameras and camcorders. The project began in earnest in 1973, under the guidance of Kazuo Iwama, who became the president of Sony in 1976 and was the main inspiration behind it. Step-by-step, hurdle-by-hurdle, the team kept moving on, and in 1980 was able to produce the world's first CCD camera, the XC-1. The pride of the company, it was mounted on an All Nippon Airways (ANA) jumbo jet to project images from the cockpit at the departure and landing times into the cabins.

However, it was produced in a limited quantity and the company engineers needed to travel a long road to achieve the degree of perfection and sensitivity they had been aiming for. The device in hand was a 120,000-pixel CCD camera, and the challenge was to increase the number of the pixels on it as far as possible. Apart from the technical issues, one of the main challenges was to ensure a super-clean, dust-free manufacturing environment as even dust particles measuring a few microns would affect the product quality. As they got on to it in the coming years, with their dedication and resolve, the team was able to achieve the goal they had set, and in January 1985 were able to introduce the 250,000-pixel CCD, 8 mm camcorder.

This was a major milestone in this direction, and nobody would've been happier and prouder on this day than Iwama, who had been the guiding light of the project. But unfortunately, during the course of its development, in 1982, he had taken ill and passed away in August of the same year. As a tribute to his dedication to this development, Norio Ohga, who had succeeded him as the president, took a chip from the first lot and affixed it on the back of his tombstone with the words, 'Iwama-san, we've finally succeeded in the mass production of the CCDs you promoted.'

As the quality of picture resolution depended on the number of pixels on the chip, the race was on to increase the number of pixels. The company aimed for the next camcorder with a 3,80,000-pixel chip but began to encounter dust problems, which had started to affect the quality and yield. In time, many such problems were resolved and there was progressive improvement in the number of pixels on the CCD and in the efficiency of the devices. In the early 1990s, the company was able to introduce chips with two million pixels per inch, 4,10,000 pixels per half inch and 4,10,000 pixels per quarter inch. A chip one-third of an inch in size was introduced, and lenses as small as seven microns, called 'on-chip lenses', were produced. Over time, the CCD became a major semiconductor business for Sony, and the component was supplied to many OEMs (original equipment manufacturers).

Computer Forays

Although Sony had made some major contributions in the digital arena, it was unable to make much headway in the computer-related activities. Perhaps one of the reasons was that there had previously been resistance within the company to this effect, as the senior management feared it would make them deviate from their core competencies of semiconductors and consumer electronics and dissipate energies in a different direction. Moreover, from the 1980s onwards, there had been a huge upsurge, an exponential growth, in the computer field in the US, with an increasing number of players joining the fray, making the whole game fiercely competitive.

It is creditable for the company that despite these factors, it was able to achieve moderate successes in its different ventures. To begin with, the electronic Abacus research for which Ibuka had reprimanded Uemura, did get to see the light of day. The experimental model of the ICC-500 SOBAX, the desktop calculator appeared in the market in June 1967. A precursor to the modern electronic calculators, perhaps it had made its appearance a little before its time. As accounting firms had been used to mechanical calculators, they found it inconvenient to switch to this new heavy device. On the other hand, which housewife would use a 270,000-yen calculator for keeping household accounts? Yet, it was much appreciated in the technical circles because of its advanced features, and eventually even found its place as a display item in the Smithsonian Institution in Washington DC.

Initial ventures aside, it was only in the early 1980s when the computer age was upon the world, that the company began to take some serious steps in this direction. One of the first efforts by Sony in this space was a dual offering: Series-35, an English-language word processor, and a portable 'Typecorder' typewriter, in December 1980. Both products featured liquid crystal display (LCD) systems and were targeted at the US market. Subsequently in December 1982, the SMC-70 series of microcomputers with high-quality graphic capability was introduced. But with increasing competition driven by innovation in the US, these products couldn't achieve the expected sales in the international market. A later product, NEWS (Network Engineering Work Station) however can be termed as a moderate success as it was well-received in the market. Introduced in January 1987, NEWS was designed for use as an automated design tool like CAD (Computer Aided Design) systems. Highly cost-effective and efficient compared to similar systems, it became popular among university students and laboratory researchers for designing, editing and developing software, till competition began to take over.

Although Sony could not make waves in the computer hardware field, it remained a major innovator in certain software-related areas. One of the significant contributions of the company to the computer world around this time has been the 3.5-inch MFD (micro floppy disc) and drive. The project began with an objective to produce a better alternative to the conventional 5.25-inch floppy disc, with a magnetic film in a resin cover, being used at the time. After experimenting with different materials and sizes, the design team finally came up with a

3.5-inch MFD, comprising a 3.4 mm thick plastic shell with one megabyte capacity, in 1980. It was a major breakthrough at a time when many manufacturers had been engaged in developing products along similar lines. Soon there was a competition between Sony's floppy disc and a three-inch disc developed by Matsushita, Hitachi and Maxwell, besides some others. Since Sony's disc offered double the storage capacity along with other plus points, it was preferred by many leading computer manufacturers like HP, Apple and later even IBM. Eventually, it became the industry standard after being formally approved by ISO (International Organization for Standardization) in 1984.

Although Sony had withdrawn from the PC market in the 1980s on account of the tepid response to its computers, it re-entered the fray in 1996 by introducing the Vaio (Visual Audio Intelligent Organizer) brand of desktop computers. To set it apart from others, it offered 3D graphical interface. The following year, it came out with its exclusive Vaio laptops that were 'super slim', encased in a four-panel magnesium body. In 2001, Steve Jobs presented to the Sony executives a Vaio running on the Mac O/S, with a suggestion to collaborate. But since Windows was more popular, Sony decided to play safe and go with Microsoft. Ultimately, Vaio was unable to get significant market share, and the company decided to sell off the Vaio computer division to Japan Industrial Partners in 2014.

THE CHALLENGE OF CHANGE

Change, as they say, is the only constant in this world. So, just as the world had turned a new corner in the beginning of the 1950s, it was again time for it to turn a new leaf in the beginning of the 1980s. For Sony, it meant changes at various levels — not just on the domestic and international commercial front, but also at their own organizational level.

From the 1950s onwards, the world had entered a different era, especially in the advanced nations. The main reason for this was the technological and industrial growth, which in turn brought about a variety of changes. Volume production also meant lowering of costs and greater affordability. This led to a greater demand for goods and services, with consumerism becoming the order of the day. This development interestingly had an impact on another area. To encourage talent and creativity, a climate of open systems was favoured, which consequently led to an increasing number of women joining the workforce. Greater independence and empowerment of women would later have an impact on the demography of such countries, and thus on the economy.

In this scenario, motivated by a new energy and enthusiasm, Japan had begun to make deep inroads into the world markets, especially the US and western Europe. Automotive majors such as Mitsubishi, Toyota, Honda and Suzuki, and the electronic sector comprising National Panasonic, Sharp, JVC, Akai, Sanyo, Sony, etc. with their quality offerings, had started to capture the international markets—even overriding well-established brands like Ford Motors, General Motors, General Electric and many others. As there was an increasing demand of products, companies generally preferred long-term planning, often with additional debt obligations and extra capacity. Moreover, imbued in the traditional value system, most of the Japanese firms generally hired employees for life.

All this had worked well, as long as the demand had been increasing. But in the mid-1980s, after a boom of over 30 years, things began to slow down in the US and in western Europe. The main reason for this slowdown was the fact that it is generally difficult to maintain such momentum beyond a point as the 'law of averages' begins to catch up. Further, the economic empowerment of women had begun to have a direct impact on the birth rate of these countries. The obvious question is how would a working woman balance the home and work life while bringing up a large number of children? All these factors meant a decrease in demand for goods in the market.

Previously, on account of expansion and growth, the demand for capital in Japan had been high and the bank rates had started to come down. Also, with companies doing well, their stocks had begun to appreciate with more and more money finding its way into the stock market. But as the demand slowed down, the industry started to suffer and banks began to face defaults. This had a domino effect on the economy, and a slump followed. Many experts and economists have called it Japan's 'lost decade' that lasted till 2002.

New Markets, New Opportunities

Interestingly, as the Japanese economy and those of the Western countries began to slow down (in case of the US, IT was a saving grace), in the mid-1980s, some new developments began to act as counterbalancing forces. China and the Soviet Union that had earlier adopted the communist model of economy, by the 1980s began to collapse due to inherent contradictions, and the Berlin Wall came down in 1989. Further, a large number of countries with sizeable economies, in Asia and elsewhere – Brazil, India, South Africa, Indonesia, Malaysia, Thailand, Vietnam, Bangladesh, etc. – called the emerging markets, had begun to liberalize their economies and revise protectionist policies, and join the rest of the world in trade and commerce. So, while earlier about half of the world could call itself part of the free-trade market, now practically the whole world was open for business.

However, for any industry or country, the opening up of new markets is a double-edged sword. For the established players, it means new markets to sell their products, but also in the long run indicates greater competition in everything – manufacturing, marketing, product development, innovation, etc. The local player of course wouldn't just sit back and watch while being taken advantage of, and would inevitably join the race to collaborate or compete, seek a licence from the foreign entity or produce a clone of its own. Thus, as the world began to open up, it meant more and more competition for the earlier big industry players like Japan, Germany, France, the US and the UK.

On the whole, it was also a win-win situation for everybody—an atmosphere of competition and cooperation and sharing of know-how, technology, materials and men benefitting all. A relevant example in this context is that of Maruti Suzuki India Ltd, which was set up in 1982 to market and produce cars in India. In 2020, the company had 53 per cent market share of the Indian car market. Suzuki Motor Corporation owns 56.21 per cent of the Indian subsidiary.

The macro picture aside, for Sony too it was to be new era in many ways. For about 30 years after its inception, it had grown on the back of its innovations in audio and visual consumer products. These were its core competencies. These basic concepts would always have their mass appeal, but then the format of offering can change and the mode of transmission can be new.

As developments in different fields had created certain momentum, new inventions and innovations had begun to appear at a fast pace. The invention of the transistor had led to the IC, which in turn formed the basis of the microprocessor. These developments heralded the digital age.

Sony, always determined to keep up with the times, had to contend with these new changes. In fact, there was much discussion within the organization as to how far to venture into the digital arena. In times marked by fast innovation and obsolescence, you can't run the risk of being irrelevant. Rightly enough, Sony didn't want to become another IBM, Apple or Microsoft, as its areas of interest were different, but would keep itself aligned with the latest developments in technology and contribute towards those in whatever way possible. In the preceding chapter, we've discussed at length how Sony took on the digital challenge and contributed towards it in a major way. High-end computer-related activities eluded it though as the IT field had started to become practically an ocean and called for greater degree of involvement.

Economy has its own dynamics and will continue to go with the flow of the market forces. For Sony, meanwhile, it was to be another different type of change to be dealt with. The company had begun operation in 1946 and since then, both Ibuka and Morita had presided over its operation with great flourish and aplomb. Having steered the company through an eventful journey, marked by a series of successes despite some setbacks, Ibuka decided to take a back seat in 1976, handing over the chairmanship to Morita. Although Morita had, for about two decades at the helm of affairs, taken some major decisions (like acquisition of CBS, Hollywood studios, etc.), it was becoming clear to everyone that the responsibility to take the company into the next millennium would now devolve onto the new-generation executives.

The next chapter will analyse in detail how the transition from the old guard to the new took place, and how the new leaders rose to the occasion to take the legacy of their founders forward.

LIFE AFTER FOUNDERS

In 1976 Ibuka had decided to divest himself of the major responsibilities, and take a back seat. Morita became the chairman in his place and continued till 1994, when he formally resigned due to failing health. The next incumbent, Norio Ohga, was an old Sony hand, and had practically grown up with the company. Given his track record and sense of involvement, he was the right choice and quite capable of carrying the legacy of the founders forward, and taking the company into the next millennium.

The world had opened up like never before, and there was increasing competition in every field. Under these circumstances, the company, weighing its strengths and options, adopted a two-pronged approach: continue to build on its core competencies like semiconductors and consumer electronics, and steadily expand into new areas of activity. Sony, under the leadership of Morita, had acquired CBS Records in 1988 and Columbia Pictures in 1989. It had also started expanding into video games and financial services like banking and insurance.

Let's take a look at how it fared in its ventures from the 1990s onwards, sans founders.

AIBO, PlayStation et al.

In the new area of IT, Sony's position had been quite clear since the beginning. While it was never its intention to become a full-fledged IT company, it would definitely cash in on the new opportunities being presented by it and utilize its talent and skills to the best of its ability therein.

The chapter 'Going Digitial' notes how Sony's performances in this new technology had been more or less satisfactory. And in the early 1990s, it chanced upon a new opportunity that was to give it one of its future star products. Since the company had previously developed CDs in collaboration with Philips, it was approached by Nintendo, a Japanese video games manufacturing company, in 1991, to help it produce the CD-ROM for one of its gaming systems, Super Famicom. Towards the end of the project, the two had developed differences over revenue sharing, and the collaboration was called off.

Subsequently, Sony started its own project under the supervision of Ken Kutaragi, who had been in charge of one of Sony's hardware divisors, and was later dubbed as 'The Father of the PlayStation'. The first PlayStation was released in December 1994 in Japan, and due to its lower price point vis-à-vis rival Sega Saturn, drew heavy response and sales. Later, it was released elsewhere in the world and steadily began to climb the sales charts. Whether it was because of the talent of developers, the vision of the company or anything else, the product was a major hit, with the original console of any type to ship over 100 million units under a decade. Starting from the PlayStation 1, with offerings such as home consoles, handheld and micro consoles, the company has gone on to release next-generation gadgets going up to PlayStation 5 as of 2021.

It has often been ahead of the competition, recording impressive sales figures: PlayStation 2, released in 2000, remains the best-selling home console, with 155 million units sold worldwide till the end of 2012; PlayStation 3, released in 2006, sold over 87.4 million units by March 2017; and PlayStation 4 launched in 2013 sold over a million units in a single day, setting a new record of sorts. Keeping up with this tradition, in November 2020, the company came out with the PlayStation 5. It has been an ongoing profitable venture of Sony with constant upgradations and innovations that offer avid gamers enhanced and richer gaming experience and thrills—with thousands of choices ranging from 007 Racing, 101 Dalmatians II: Patch's London Adventure, 2002 FIFA World Cup, 3 Xtreme to 5 Star Racing, Ace Combat 2, Ball Breakers, Barbie: Explorer and many more.

Another interactive-digital offering made by Sony around this time was AIBO (Artificial Intelligence Robot) that was first launched on 11 May 1999. New models were released every year till 2006, but on account of tepid response, the company even stopped providing back-up services like repairs in July 2014. With revival of interest in the concept within the company and in the larger interest of innovation, the project was reintroduced in November 2017, and the fourth-generation model was launched in Japan in January 2018. As robotics and Artificial Intelligence (AI) would be the technologies of future, the experience and expertise gathered while developing AIBO would come in handy for the Sony engineers.

Music and Films

Akio Morita was born in a family inclined towards classical music, and his was one of the few families in the country to own an RCA Victrola. Another important Sony old-timer, Norio Ohga, had been a baritone and an alumnus of Tokyo National University of Fine Arts of Music. Both had a strong passion for music and felt an expansion in the area would also complement their current operation. In the 1960s, under pressure from different quarters, the government had relaxed rules about foreign investment in Japan. As a result of this, Sony was able to form a joint venture with CBS, called CBS-Sony, in 1968. The new music company, under the leadership of Ohga, showed a lot of promise and grew from a small subsidiary into an independent profit-making venture, rewarding employees with bonuses thrice a year, and declaring high dividends. In 1988, the company celebrated its 20th anniversary, and was proud to declare that from a 700-million-yen revenue in the first year, it had been able to register sales of 110 billion yen per year.

In the late 1980s when the situation was different and the company was looking to expand, the CBS acquisition appeared to be a promising business idea. In a way it was an extension and enhancement of the process that had begun in 1968. After protracted deliberations stretching over a year, Sony was able to acquire CBS Records in 1988, with all their assets and liabilities. The new company was christened Sony Music. The company has traversed a long journey in its 30 years of operation marked by successes and setbacks, and with its own share of controversies.

In the early 2000s, Sony Music got some bad press due to their dispute with Michael Jackson, who was waiting for the 'masters' of his albums to be reverted to him, enabling him to promote them as he desired. He was surprised to see the 'date of reverting' set to some time in future. He thought he had been shortchanged by the company and sought an early exit from his contract with Sony. Jackson also had had some issues with the then Sony Music chairman Tommy Mottola, whom he had accused of being racist. Later in February 2016, music artist Kesha levelled rape charges against music producer Dr Luke and sought early release from her contract with the company. Her plea was rejected by the New York City Supreme Court.

Having been among the 'Big Three', along with Universal Music Group and Warner Music for long, the company has become No. 1, the largest publisher of music in the world as of 2021. On 14 November 2018, it acquired about 60 per cent equity in EMI Music Publishing, and combined with the 40 per cent share it already held, EMI became its wholly owned subsidiary, making Sony numero uno in the music world. Engaged in almost all aspects of music production, publishing and distribution, Sony Music's list of labels covers the who's who of the music industry, ranging from Beyonce, Ricky Martin, Mariah Carey, Britney Spears and Frank Sinatra to Shakira, Alan Walker, Prince, Celine Dion, Whitney Houston, Alicia Keys and more. With an annual revenue upwards of $7 billion, it has been contributing about 10 per cent to the overall revenue of Sony Corporation in recent years.

Compared to the CBS Records deal, Sony's acquisition of Columbia Pictures in 1989 was a much smoother affair. Once the company had made up its mind and the stakeholders were on board, the deal didn't take much time, except for discussions about the management of the new company. With this deal, Tri-Star Pictures also came under the Sony banner, in which Columbia had a large stake.

The deal was essentially managed and concluded by Ohga, though Morita, who was the chairman at the time, was the driving force behind it. Morita and others felt that acquisition of major music and film businesses would complement their hardware operation. Also, Morita felt if they had had a big studio with them earlier, they wouldn't have lost out on the Beta war. In the late 1980s, when even a million dollars was a large amount, Sony's acquisition of the studio at $3.4 billion was one of the biggest deals of the time, creating ripples not just in the US but also in Japan. Many analysts felt that the company had overpaid for the takeover, and Sony, who prided their business suaveness, would soon get a reality check.

As Sony was new to the films operation, they relied heavily on some old Hollywood hands, and even got embroiled in costly fights with Warner Bros. for poaching their executives. Worse, the new managers, flush with cash, in their enthusiasm, produced some very expensive films that bombed at the box office. Five years down the line, in 1994, the company was embarrassed to announce a major loss on account of this acquisition. Having learnt the ropes gradually, the unit started getting on its feet, and the operations began to stabilize.

In a few years' time, it was able to produce one of the biggest blockbusters of all time, *Spider-Man*, in 2002 that grossed $821.7 million against a budget of $139 million. In possession of the *Spider-Man* rights, subsequently, the studio produced two *Spider-Man* series till 2014: the *Spider-Man* trilogy of films, from 2002 to 2007, starring Tobey Maguire, and the *Amazing Spider-Man* films, from 2012 to 2014, starring Andrew Garfield. Its other successes have been *The Karate Kid, Ghostbusters, Jumanji, Stuart Little, Men in Black, Hotel Transylvania, Charlie's Angels* and more. In 2021, it is part of the Big Five of Hollywood, along with Walt Disney Studios, Warner Bros., Universal Pictures and Paramount Pictures. A major profit-making unit, it contributed $9.32 billion towards the group's revenues in 2020.

Insurance and Bank

As business on the domestic front had begun to stabilize towards late 1950s, Morita had started to travel to the US to look for more avenues of growth. On one such visit, he was rather struck by an impressive, imposing high-rise in Chicago. On inquiring, he found that it was the office of Prudential Insurance. 'Why would a life insurance company have such an enormous building?' he wondered.

And then he told himself, 'One day, we will establish our own bank or financial institution and build a building like that' — a dream he kept harbouring from then on. That was the germinating idea of Sony Insurance and his wish was granted in 1981 when the company started a joint venture in Japan with Prudential Financial Inc., a large US insurance company. There were 23 insurance companies in Japan (led by giants like Daichi and Nippon), while the US had over 1,800 firms. The Ministry of Finance was somewhat reluctant to allow a non-financial company like Sony to enter the field as it would prompt others to make their bid too. Additionally, there was much opposition from other insurance companies too, as they feared that the entry of an American megacorporation would affect their business.

Despite these issues, Morita was able to convince the Ministry of his point of view, arguing that in the ultimate analysis an insurance instrument too was after all like a product. One step closer to realizing his dream, the operations were launched with much enthusiasm and fanfare. 'Starting today, life insurance will change and "Life Planners" will change it,' read a newspaper ad at the launch.

While the other companies traditionally employed salesladies to market insurance, Sony went for more professional 'Life Planners'. Under this innovative model, the planners were given much freedom and flexibility in their operation. They were virtually 'owners' of their businesses, employed their staff and secretaries, and worked on salary or commission basis, depending upon their competence and business. Further, the company had an edge over others. It was backed by aggressive marketing and was able to focus more on the specific needs of the individuals and thus offer them custom-designed products.

Although, with the dedication and commitment of the management and the planners, the business had started to grow. In 1987, Prudential expressed a desire to pull out to establish its own fully owned subsidiary in Japan. After further negotiations with the Ministry, Prudential decided to go its own way, while still retaining 30 per cent share in Sony's company. Consequently, Sony Prudential Life Insurance thus became Sony Pruco Life Insurance in September 1987.

In 1991, Sony-Pruco celebrated its 10th anniversary with a total insurance portfolio exceeding two trillion yen and total assets of 90 billion yen, and the company's name too was officially changed to Sony Life Insurance Co. Ltd. In March 1993, it recorded its first non-consolidated fiscal year profit. As of 2020, it is part of Sony Financial Holdings Ltd, and contributes substantially towards the company's overall revenue.

In June 2001, Sony also came to establish a bank. Unlike conventional banks, it is a direct bank with no physical branches or ATMs anywhere. In fact, the concept of a direct bank has been gaining some traction with an increase in digitization and internet services in the recent years.

Sony Bank is one of the largest online banks in Japan offering financial services involving foreign currency deposits, investment trusts and home loans. It had a net income of 6.6 billion yen in 2019.

Batteries

As we've seen in Sony's life story, it was always open to strategic collaborations and affiliations with other companies for mutual benefit. In the 1970s, their product range and volume had started to grow substantially, and for their battery requirement, they had to rely on domestic manufacturers. Ibuka and Morita thought it to be a good idea to have their own battery manufacturing facility, which besides meeting their own captive requirement could also tap into the growing domestic market.

Following this, in 1975, Sony set up a joint venture called Sony-Eveready Inc. in collaboration with Union Carbide, US, for the marketing and manufacturing of batteries in Japan. It was planned to first market the batteries imported from the US under the Sony-Eveready brand name, and later manufacture the same in the country. Within three years, Sony's Koriyama, Fukushima battery plant was operationalized and domestic production had started. The operation continued smoothly under the tie-up for over a decade till March 1986, when due to certain concerns the collaborations had to be terminated.

The unit was renamed Sony Energytec Inc. and it continued to engage in R&D activities, independent of Union Carbide. Within four years, it was able to produce the world's first lithium-ion rechargeable battery, which had been Morita's dream. In 2000, the unit was merged with Sony Motomiya, to form Sony Fukushima, which again in 2004 merged with Sony Tochigi to become Sony Energy Devices Corporation. The new entity carried on with its battery and energy-related operation until 2016 when it agreed to transfer its battery business to Murata Manufacturing Co. Ltd. The unit currently manages the sales department of Sony-branded consumer battery products and some other operations.

Going Forward in Tough Times

When it comes to a company like Sony, a comparison between its earlier era, and the post-founders' phase is but natural. In 1994, Morita resigned as the chairman, making way for Norio Ohga. Since then, till 2020, the company has seen five CEOs, including Ohga. While conducting an orchestra in Beijing on 7 November 2001, Ohga suffered a cerebral hemorrhage and collapsed on stage. Although he recovered his ability to speak and move after a three-month coma, he decided to step down in favour of Nobuyuki Idei, who remained at the helm till 2005. Idei was replaced by the British-born American, Sir Howard Stringer.

Incidentally, Stringer was perhaps the first American to head a major Japanese company. Seven years hence, in 2012, he made way for one of his favourites, Kazuo Hirai, who took over as the president and CEO—one of the reasons for his selection being his facility in both Japanese and English. Hirai held this position till April 2018, when he became the chairman and served in this capacity till June 2019. He was replaced by his long-time deputy Kenichiro Yoshida, who continues in the capacity of CEO as of 2020.

Comparing the general performance of the company between the two phases (founders' and post-founders' time) makes for an interesting study. Sony had registered a steady rise in its performance from the 1960s onwards, dominating the marketplace like a colossal a few decades later. If Sony's revenue was $51.55 million in 1961, it went up to $414.36 million in 1970, and then to $4.23 billion in 1980. In 1990, it was $18.34 billion and in 2000, it had touched a peak of $63.08 billion. In one decade, the business had risen by over 350 per cent, which was unprecedented for any large company.

From here onwards however, it was to be a different story for Sony. As discussed earlier, besides many internal factors affecting the company, the world had opened up and there was increasing competition in the market. Consequently, in the subsequent years, it was to be a slow progress for it, with the overall revenue rising by a mere 40 per cent in the entire decade to $86.52 billion in 2010. The slide continued, and the sales touched a low of $67.89 billion in 2016. The company had not turned a profit since 2008, and Sony's share price in April 2012 had hit rock-bottom, keeping in the range of $15–18, a quarter of its value a decade earlier.

'How the Tech Parade Passed Sony By', ran the headline of an article in *The New York Times*,[6] describing the reasons for Sony's poor show. The main reason for this decline, as indicated in the report, was that while the company was hit hard on its regular business of consumer electronics, it had been slow in reinventing itself to adapt to changes. Sony's TV business, which used to be its mainstay, had not turned in profit from 2004 onwards, and losses on that count had gradually risen to a total of over $4.6 billion by 2013. Many new players had come into the fray. There were the Korean brands such as Samsung and LG, and the Chinese led by TCL, Hisense, Haier and others. Increasing competition meant heavy cost cutting and induction of new technologies. Sony, which prided itself on quality offerings, began to lose out in the price war. It was late to introduce the new technology of the flat screen and was beset with other woes.

It's argued that while the companies like Samsung and Apple focused essentially on a handful of products (TVs, computers and smartphones) and on improving quality therein, Sony's TV and camcorder catalogues presented a very confusing picture—with over 10 camcorder models and 30 different colour TVs on the offer. Most of its managers worked in silos without much coordination and communication with the other departments. And then there was the issue of new technologies. Analysts opine that the company had not shown the agility to ride the digital wave quick enough to present smart new products such as the iPod or iTunes. It had been too preoccupied with the hardware to develop new skills in software. Despite its vast music and film assets and other resources, it failed to capitalize on fresh opportunities. Why hadn't it thought of going the Netflix way, or introduce devices for streaming music earlier on in the day—were some simple questions being asked. It was also suggested that the language and culture differences between the CEO Stringer and the top executives during this time contributed to the general downturn too.

On 27 May 2013, another news report in *The New York Times*, with a headline, 'Sony's Bread and Butter? It's not Electronics',[7] talked of Sony's ailing electronics business, and referred to many analysts advising Sony the way forward. Hedge fund manager, Daniel S. Loeb, felt that Sony could ideally spin off the profitable part of its movies and music business and raise cash to revive the electronics business. Some others felt the company was better off selling insurance and making music and films, rather than electronic devices. Atul Goyal, a fund manager from Jefferies, went a step further and said, 'Electronics is its Achilles' heel and, in our view, it is worth zero... In our view, it needs to exit most electronic markets.'

Share market analysts have a different view from those of company executives who have nurtured their favourite products with their blood and sweat. The chief executive Kazuo Hirai, who took office in

2012, would not even dream of exiting the electronics business. 'Electronics has a future,' he said. 'And it's in Sony's DNA.' He had made sound plans for the turnaround. In November 2013, he brought Kenichiro Yoshida into the front ranks from one of Sony's Internet units, and in 2015 made him the CFO of the company. Yoshida, having spent 30 years of his career in different capacities in Sony, had a sound insider-understanding of the company's working. Using his new mandate, he went about cutting jobs, sold off the iconic Vaio computer business, spun out its TV set unit and curtailed the company's involvement in smartphone-related activities. His cost-cutting measures and focused approach began to show positive results with things improving for the company again. In recent years, not only has its traditional TV market begun to pick up, but new forays in robotics and AI also promise bright prospects, as detailed in a following chapter.

MASARU IBUKA—HELPING SHAPE A NEW JAPAN

asaru Ibuka was born on 11 April 1908 in the beautiful town of Nikko, in Tochigi Prefecture (district) of Japan, about 100 km north of Tokyo. His father, a Protestant Christian from the island of Hokkaido, had graduated from the Department of Electrical Engineering at Hokkaido University, and later worked in a copper refinery in Nikko, where Ibuka was born. His grandfather, Motoi, had grown up a samurai in the Aizu fief (about 300 km from Tokyo) and had risen through the ranks of civil service to the position of provincial deputy governor in his time. According to some accounts, his father had played a key role in building Japan's first-ever hydroelectric power plant. Unfortunately, he passed away in a tragic electrocution accident when Ibuka was just two. Following this, his mother took him to his paternal grandparents in Kobe, about 524 km from Tokyo. Later when his mother remarried, he stayed back with his grandparents and was brought up by them.

Perhaps it was because of the science-genes of the family, that right from his childhood he showed immense interest and curiosity in all things mechanical and electrical. Whenever he would come across a toy, a watch or some gadget, he would try to take it apart and study its internal mechanism. One could say that the screwdriver was one of his favourite tools. When he was a young boy, he would often visit one of their old family friends, the Kiharas' home in Hakodate, Hokkaido (869 km from Tokyo). Upon hearing about his arrival, the people at home would scramble to hide such things as clocks, toys and small items warning others, 'Master Masaru is here.'

At home too, when he would dismantle such items and then wouldn't be able to put them back together, his indulgent grandfather would bring him new ones to take apart again. In fact, this habit persisted throughout his life, and perhaps also played a key role in making him the innovator that he turned out to be. In John Nathan's book, *Sony: The Private Life*, Ibuka's son, Makoto, talks of his father's passion for toys and recalls that whenever one of them (Ibuka or Morita) returned from a trip abroad, there would be one bag full of actual toys from F.A.O Schwarz. But those would be given to children only after they had been taken apart and reassembled, or partially reassembled. And according to Morita's second son, Masao, a visit to one of the founders' offices was like 'stepping inside a toy box'.[8]

Following his natural inclination towards science and technology, Ibuka joined the prestigious Waseda University in Tokyo and graduated with an electrical engineering degree in 1933. He began his career with a company called PCL (Photo-chemical Laboratories), where he had been exposed to the process of recording and developing motion picture films. When he lost interest in it, the promoter Taiji Uemura transferred him to another of his companies, where he worked on optical sound, from 1937 to 1940. Later, Uemura formed Japan Measuring Instruments and made Ibuka the managing director of this new set-up. Ibuka continued here till 1945 when he decided to go on his own.

Magnetic Personality

As far as his professional achievements are concerned, they have been discussed at length elsewhere in the book. Here, we'd like to focus on his personal attributes which made him an exceptional leader and one of the most respected names in business internationally.

We find that at least two major qualities in his personality stand out and made him the businessman that he was: Ibuka's confidence in his own technical capabilities, and a natural talent for attracting people and the ability to take them along—a truly formidable combination! We've seen that following his incorrigible tinkering habit and interest in science he had been able to earn an engineering degree for himself—and not just that, while in college one of his discoveries, a form of the element Neon with applications in transmission of light, won a prize at an international science fair at Paris. Impressed by his achievements, some of his fellow students and teachers even called him a 'student inventor of genius'. Referring to his achievements, a headline in a Tokyo newspaper read: 'Basking in the light of international recognition: a genius inventor'. From then on, his successes in the technological field kept on reaffirming his faith in his capabilities—the feeling that 'I can do it!' and 'It will work out somehow.'

So, from the initial success of the tape recorder to the transistor radio, transistor TV and going up to Betamax and Betacam, despite facing hurdles and overcoming them with ingenuity, the company was able to earn the epithet of 'innovator,' mainly because of the driving spirit of Ibuka. At the time of developing the colour TV when the Chromatron cost overruns and technical problems were making the project unviable, he didn't lose hope. As though he was pulling a rabbit out of his hat, he was able to guide the technical team out of the dire straits and launch Trinitron that became a worldwide sensation. Ibuka's self-confidence in inspiring his people and ability in managing difficult situations, contributed in no small measure to making his company what it became.

Apart from his technical competence and capabilities, another major quality that brought him success was his humane approach to issues. In his *Founding Prospectus*, he had clearly stated that the objective behind setting up the company was to help his people realize their full potential by creating 'a stable work environment where engineers who had a deep and profound appreciation for technology could realize their societal mission and work to their heart's content.' 'We shall distribute the company's surplus earnings to all employees in an appropriate manner, and we shall assist them in a practical manner to secure a stable life,' the *Prospectus* further stated. No surprise then that a lot of talented people made a life-long career with the company and contributed towards its growth whole-heartedly.

Much has been written about his relationship with Akio Morita, but there are two other important associations that also need to be mentioned — those with Kazuo Iwama and Norio Ohga. With the support of Ibuka and Morita, both made major contributions in building the company since its fledgling days.

Kazuo Iwama, born in 1919 in Nagoya, was a geophysicist who worked at the Earthquake Research Institute of Tokyo University before joining the company. Morita and he had been neighbours in the Shirakabe district of Nagoya and the two had known each other well for long. Iwama was also engaged to be married to Morita's younger sister Kikuko since the war. Morita persuaded him to join Totsuko when the company was established in 1946. Iwama's contributions to the company's progress remained immense and far-reaching.

Once the transistor licence had been acquired, the company didn't have much to go by, except a compilation of technical details and facts by the Western Electric engineers in the form of a book, *Transistor Technology*. Iwama spent over three months in the US, studying the manufacture of transistor at the Western Electric plants and other locations, and sent home detailed notes and diagrams for people to work on. Progress on the transistor technology by the company was largely owing to his committed efforts. He was also the driving force behind the innovations in CCD that was used for making digital cameras and camcorders. The research in that field proved path-breaking, resulting in a range of benefits for the company in the long run.

Norio Ohga's first interface with the company happened in the early 1950s when he was a young student of Tokyo National University of Fine Arts and Music. A music student and also interested in acoustic technology, he was keen to introduce the tape recorder into the music-learning curriculum. However, he found many faults in Sony's first tape recorder which he thought could be corrected by further development. Impressed by his knowledge of music and technology, Ibuka let him get involved in the production processes, and he was made a part-time consultant. To fuel his passion, he went on to study music in Munich and Berlin, where he also formed a friendship with Herbert von Karajan, one of the greatest musicians of the modern times. Over time, with his musical talents and technical knowledge, he had become an asset for Sony, and was appointed executive director at the age of 34, in 1964. He was instrumental in the development of the CD with Philips, and the driving force behind Sony's collaboration with CBS, and later its acquisition. He was appointed president of Sony in 1982 and the CEO in 1989. After Morita's resignation in 1994, he became the chairman of Sony.

These examples suggest that Ibuka's approach was always to provide a conducive and open environment for people with talent to function and flourish—they would be allowed their space to come up with new ideas which could even blossom into full-fledged, revolutionary breakthrough products. His capacity to build relationships and take people along is amply demonstrated by such life-long business relations he formed that took the company to ever newer heights.

In *Sony: The Private Life*, Nathan also throws some light on Ibuka's emotional side. Many people were not earlier aware that Ibuka was extremely attached to his mother, Sawa, and regretted the fact that he had not been able to spend sufficient time with her while being busy building a career for himself. In 1937, one year after his own marriage, he received a call from his stepfather in Tokyo that she had taken seriously ill. He took the first overnight train to Kobe from Tokyo (522.2 km), but arrived too late. He was unable to step onto Kobe for more than 10 years after the incident. In a memoir, he wrote, 'For years after I got out of college I was working so hard that I neglected her... If only she were alive now I'd bring her anything she wanted to make her happy, any treasure she could name.'[9]

In 1936, Ibuka married Sekiko Maeda, daughter of Tamon Maeda, a former diplomat and politician, and an extremely influential man with extensive contacts—who also helped Ibuka a great deal in his business later. The couple had three children: Shizuko, a daughter born in 1937; Takeko, second daughter born in 1940; and Makoto, a son born in 1945. Takeko had a normal childhood until the age of six, when she began to show some signs of mental handicap, which prevented her from attending a regular school. Ibuka, who was extremely fond of her, was shattered. Speaking of her, he would often say, 'She is the cross I bear, and the light of my life.' He later established a facility in northern Japan, called 'House of Hope', where she lived from 1973 onwards.

Although Sekiko was a talented and sensitive woman and an accomplished painter, she was not an easy person to deal with. By many different accounts, she was temperamental and a high-strung person, who found it difficult to handle sustained pressure of any kind. Ibuka, generally cool and composed, was cast in a different mould. Their divergent natures probably widened the rift between them over the years, and the marriage eventually ended in a divorce.

During his early years in Hokkaido, Ibuka had known one Yoshiko Kurasawa, daughter of a distant relative by marriage. Ibuka's mother, a great beauty herself, wished the two to be married, as Ibuka liked her, and she was one of the three 'beautiful Kurosawa girls', as known in the family circles. At that time, however, it was not to be—but the situation had changed after his divorce. Following this development, Ibuka decided to tie the knot with Yoshiko (after a waiting period of 30 years) and made news for a 'non-electronic' reason. He was called 'the last romantic to be born in the Meiji era' by some for this unusual move in a conservative, traditional society like the Japanese.

Electronics, of course, was his driving passion, but his talents extended to writing too. In the early 1970s, when he had gone into a semi-retirement mode and had begun to enjoy more leisure time, he penned around 10 books. In two of his early books, *The Zero-Year Child* (1970) and *Kindergarten Is Too Late* (1971), he expressed his firm views about raising children. In his opinion, the first three to four years of the child's development were crucial, and must be accorded more attention than most societies had been customarily giving. He felt, if in the formative years more attention was paid to language-learning, games, listening to sounds, observing nature and playing musical instruments, the children would develop into more wholesome and emotionally balanced personalities in their later years. He also wrote a book, *Masaru Ibuka and Soichiro Honda – Honda and Sony Origin, and Creative Dream,* on his long-time businessman friend Soichiro Honda, who like him was also a self-made man.

The old war horse had been carrying onerous responsibilities on his strong shoulders for several decades. In 1992, he collapsed with a serious attack of arrhythmia and was subsequently confined to a wheelchair. His favourite pastime during his later years was interacting with the visiting Sony executives and listening to the company reports. He passed away on Friday, 19 December 1997, at 3:38 a.m. at his home in Tokyo. The cause of death was heart failure. The 'Wake' (Japanese funeral ceremony), for the immediate family only, took place on Sunday, 21 December, followed by a private funeral on 22 December. A public ceremony by Sony Corporation was held on 21 January 1998.

Ohga, who had known him since his college days and who was the chairman at the time of Ibuka's demise, paid heartfelt condolences and tributes to his mentor and guide: 'The greatness of Masaru Ibuka was not only his ability to create profit but his way of looking at the company, from a cultural point of view. Even when there was very little profit being made by the company, he took a part of the profit to create Sony Fund for Education to promote science education among elementary and junior high school students and informal education.' Sony Corporation President Nobuyuki said, 'Mr Ibuka had been at the heart of Sony's philosophy... Sony would not have had its management resources that it has today were it not for Mr Ibuka's philosophy.'[10]

Some of his oft-quoted lines also offer us a glimpse into his philosophy of life: 'Creativity comes from looking for the unexpected and stepping outside your own experience'; 'We Japanese enjoy the simple pleasures, not extravagance. I believe a man should have a simple lifestyle—even if he can afford more'; 'The key to success for everything in business, science and technology is never to follow others'; 'Establish a place of work where engineers can feel the joy of technological innovation, be aware of their mission to society and work to their heart's content.'

Given his exceptional qualities, not only to those in his immediate circle but in the country too, he had come to be a much respected and revered figure, and was conferred with numerous honours. During his lifetime, he was honoured with: Medal of Honour with Blue Ribbon (1960); IEEE Founders Medal (1972); Order of the Sacred Treasure (1978); Order of the Rising Sun (1986); IEEE Consumer Electronics Award (1987) (named after him as Masaru Ibuka Consumers Electronics Award); Person of Cultural Merit (1989); Order of Culture (1992); Golden Pheasant Award by Scout Association of Japan

(1989); and Bronze Wolf by World Organization of the Scout Movement (1991), besides numerous others. He also served as chairman of Boy Scouts of Japan.

Ibuka and Morita—A Unique Bond

One of the secrets of Sony's success has also been the unique enduring relationship the founders shared. This, in fact, was one of the pillars on which the edifice of Sony was erected. After meeting in the Japanese War Room Committee during the war, and later joining hands in business, they had come closer to form an abiding long-lasting relationship. Despite an age difference of about 13 years, the two got on like a house on fire.

According to the family members, their relationship was like a melding of souls, something more than a friendship. 'They were closer than lovers, even Mrs Morita felt that,' recalls Ibuka's son Makoto. 'They were bound together by a tie so tight it was more like love than friendship.' Hideo Morita, elder son of Morita, says of their relationship, 'They would sit there, talking to each other, and we would listen but we had no idea what they were saying. Each one seemed to be talking his own story, different from the other's. It was like gibberish to us but they were understanding each other, and interrupting them for any reason was forbidden.'[11] Theirs was a kind of 'inner circle' which even their wives hesitated to break into.

Both had kept adjoining offices, and each one knew the other's office like the back of his hand. For instance, Ibuka would call his secretary and ask her to look for some screwdrivers in the 'third drawer of Morita's desk'. When in office, both would have lunch together in the company's dining room and would occasionally invite some other executive also to join in.

One of the reasons for their lasting relationship could be the basic differences in their personalities. While Morita was more outgoing and pragmatic, Ibuka was spontaneous and impulsive. He has often been referred to as a 'pure and simple soul' by those who knew him well. So, in a way they complemented each other's personalities. One explanation in this respect offered by Morita's son Hideo was that his father being the eldest in the family perhaps felt the need for a 'father figure', and looked upon Ibuka as a kind of 'elder brother'.

Given Ibuka's nature and personality, Morita also felt the need to protect him. Till Ibuka was in his early seventies, he used to leave the office on his own. Once in a public toilet at Tokyo railway station, a stranger who had recognized him approached him. He just wanted to say hello. Following this incident, Morita instructed the staff to ensure at least one escort accompanied Ibuka when he left office in the evening.

As the company grew, responsibilities for the two also kept growing. In the changing scenario, it was not unusual for the leaders to have disagreements about different policy matters. However, despite disagreements about one issue or the other, they never aired their differences in public and always put up a united face in front of the staff. For instance, the colour TV project using the Chromatron tube was essentially driven by Ibuka, and at one time had begun to cause enormous financial strain on the company. Morita, rather than blaming the senior partner for the error of judgment, worked in a positive way to address the situation. There were times he was not in agreement with Ibuka extending loans to some parties, but the two kept the matter between themselves.

In the beginning of the 1990s, both had begun to face health issues—Ibuka suffered a serious attack of arrhythmia in 1992 and had been confined to a wheel chair, and on 30 November 1993, while playing his usual morning game of tennis, Morita fell down, and was diagnosed with cerebral hemorrhage. The two spent the following years in rehabilitation. Of their meetings around this time, Makoto Ibuka said, 'Now when both are sick, they sit together in silence, holding hands, with tears running down their cheeks, and they're communicating without words. That's the kind of friendship they always shared.'

Indeed, it's difficult to find a parallel of such a relationship in the business world.

AKIO MORITA—JAPAN'S UNOFFICIAL AMBASSADOR

The eldest among four siblings, Akio Morita was born on 26 January 1921 in Kosugaya Village near Nagoya, capital of Aichi Prefecture (district), about 354 km from Tokyo. Being the first-born of Kyusaemon and Shuko Morita, he was expected to take over the family business and was thus trained to this effect since childhood. The Morita family had been in the sake, miso and soy sauce manufacturing business since 1665, and had Akio gone for it, he would've been the 15th generation in this line. His interests however lay elsewhere—in mathematics, physics and mechanics.

His mother's love of classical music too had seeped into his personality. Theirs was one of the few first families in Japan to own an RCA Victrola. At one point, Morita had become so engrossed in building his own ham radio that he almost flunked his school exams. Later, after concentrating on his studies for a year, he was able to secure a seat at the Imperial Osaka University, from where he graduated in physics in 1944. Having completed his studies, he joined the Imperial Japanese Navy as a sub-lieutenant and served the country during WWII. It was during his service in the navy that he made the acquaintance of Masaru Ibuka in the navy's Wartime Research Committee, where the two developed certain rapport which led to their future partnership in business.

Although both Ibuka and Morita had a firm grounding in science and technology and understood the basics of mechanical and electrical articles, over time, Ibuka came to be more involved in the technical side of operation, while Morita focused more on marketing and building a strong brand image for the company. So, in a way, while one built products, the other built the company. Despite being young, Morita had a wide horizon, and was acutely aware of Japan's limitations as a market. He knew if they wanted to grow, they needed to look beyond the borders—towards the US and western Europe, which were the most attractive markets of the time. And for that, there was a need of, not just product quality, but also a global image and presence.

Some of his personal experiences also drove home the necessity to change foreign buyers' perception of Japanese products as being of inferior quality. Around this time, except for Canon and Nikon, no other brands inspired much confidence among the foreign customers. Once on a tour of Germany, he had had a rather unsavoury experience that left an imprint on his mind. In a restaurant, he ordered an ice cream, and when the bearer brought it, he pointed to the paper parasol stuck in it, and said, 'This is from your country.'

However, after the mid-1950s, when Sony's tape recorders had been well accepted in the market and transistor radios had begun to sell well, things began to look up for the company. For Morita, it was also the right time to embark on a concerted programme to establish Sony's presence in the overseas markets. In 1955, the company had been able to make its first transistor radio, TR-52, which was still in the prototype stage. Bulova, a major US watch manufacturer, showed an interest in buying 100,000 sets and marketing them under their own brand name. The company thought, and rightly so, that since nobody knew about Sony in the US, it would be difficult to sell the product. Even then Morita was reluctant.

'Whoever heard of Sony?' Bulova's president said. 'Our brand has a worldwide reputation with 50 years of history behind it.' Although it was a very tempting offer for a fledgling company like Sony, Morita had the self-confidence to turn it down. 'In 50 years, we will have made the name Sony as famous as yours. So, it's no, thank you.' With such a global vision, Morita was unstoppable. Given his drive and passion, Sony had begun to spread its wings wider and broader with each passing year. One could say if Ibuka was managing the production and home front, Morita had begun to supervise the overseas operation.

Around this time, Japan relied on a few giant trading companies for the import and export of products. Morita decided to become more self-reliant, by building the Sony brand on one side, and increasing global presence by setting up the company's own branch offices and subsidiaries overseas, on the other. In 1957, a giant Sony neon sign, measuring 9.75 m long and 10.9 m high and weighing 2,250 kg, was put up at the prominent Sukiyabashi corner in Tokyo's upscale Ginza district. In

February 1960, Sony Corporation of America (SONAM) was established. In 1961, Sony's ADR was listed on the New York Stock Exchange and in October 1962, Sony opened its first showroom at the upmarket Fifth Avenue in New York. This was just the beginning—there was no stopping Sony. Manufacturing facilities, offices and affiliates were established all over the world, details of which have been mentioned in the chapter 'Taking on the World'. In all, over a hundred affiliates and subsidiaries had been established by the 1980s.

Committed and driven as Morita was, he took several initiatives on the personal front as well. He learnt English, and in 1963 even took his family to New York for a year to familiarize them with the American way of life. He was acutely aware of the importance of the US market for Japan and Sony—so he needed to work out a fine balance in protecting the interests of both. The Japanese companies were bringing quality affordable products into the US, and also creating employment opportunities in the country, but no country likes to be swamped by foreign goods. To reduce trade tensions between the two, he went the extra mile to bring the two countries closer. He even espoused American trade interests by supporting American exports to Japan. In the late 1960s, Sony forged a temporary collaboration with Texas Instruments, and in 1972 set up a subsidiary to export American products like Regal Cookware and Whirlpool Refrigerators to Japan. He had truly become an unofficial Japanese ambassador, not just to the US but to the rest of the world.

As Sony got established in the Western world in the 1970s, Morita had started becoming increasingly confident of airing his views, whether about American management style or Japan's protectionist policies. Despite being a nationalist, on the whole, he was trying to be fair and objective. He felt that the Japanese companies were ahead of their US counterparts because they were managed by engineers and technocrats, unlike the US companies that were run by 'general' managers, MBAs, etc. In his view, the American managers lived from one balance sheet to another — were financial paper shufflers who could see only '10 minutes ahead' — while the Japanese took a long-term view of the businesses.

He was also fairly vocal and active in opposing what he thought to be unfair trade practices. In 1984, he went around meeting many governors and then President Ronald Reagan to lobby against the Unitary Tax imposed by some of the US states, which was levied not just on a multinational company's earnings in the specific state, but on their global earnings too. An unfair tax in his view, Morita decided to retaliate and even threatened to take business out of those states that imposed this tax. He even talked of 'hollowing out' the American economy. Consequently, California and many other states abolished the tax. He wrote of the trade imbalance between the US and Japan in 1989, 'There are few things in the United States that Japan wants to buy, but there are a lot of things in Japan that Americans want to buy. This is at the root of the trade imbalance.'[12]

In 1989, he found himself at the centre of a controversy when a book co-authored by him and a prominent Japanese nationalist leader Shintaro Ishihara, *The Japan That Can Say No,*[13] got published in Japan. The book urged the nationalist Japanese to stand up to the American trade practices, which it alleged were motivated partly by racism. The book also said that Japan had the power to alter the balance of power in the world by selling its advanced computer chips to the Soviet Union rather than the US. When its unauthorized English translation found its way to the US, it raised some hackles in America. Even though the aggressive comments occurred in the chapters written by Ishihara,

Morita felt embarrassed by its publication. It is said that Morita had no intentions of criticizing the US. In a damage-control mode, he later got his chapters removed from the English version and distanced himself from the book.

On the other hand, he didn't spare his own country either. Being personally involved in the production processes and company's growth, Morita had come to believe that on-the-job training and experience were far more important and valuable for professional competence than just good college or university grades. In this respect, in 1966, he wrote a book, *Never Mind School Records*. At one point, the company had even stopped asking fresh applicants the names of their alumni, college or university. Shortly before he suffered the stroke, he stirred up a hornet's nest by commenting that his country was like a 'fortress' that had been alienating a lot of its trading partners. 'Although there's much to commend in Japan's economic system, it is simply too far out of sync with the West on certain essential points,' he wrote in *The Atlantic Monthly* in June 1993.[14] He even advocated shorter working hours for the Japanese workforce, more dividends for investors in Japanese companies and a relook at many protectionist policies.

119

His critics felt that he had become arrogant due to his fame and fortune. In a conservative society like that of the Japanese, where businessmen tend to be somewhat reticent about flaunting their wealth, he travelled in his personal corporate jet and helicopter. He even appeared in a TV commercial for American Express. Outgoing and athletic, he was a keen sportsman too. He played golf for over 40 years. Subscribing to the philosophy that it's never too late to learn anything, he took up tennis at 55, downhill skiing at 60, water skiing at 64 and scuba diving at 68. He had two sons and a daughter with his wife Yoshiko.

In 1986, he published an autobiography with the assistance of Edwin M. Reingold and Mitsuko Shimomura, *Made in Japan: Akio Morita and Sony*. The book talks about the origins of his family, Japanese history and culture and how they've impacted the Japanese way of thinking and conducting business. It also goes into details about Sony's rise to fame and fortune, growth from its early development of tape recorder to transistor radio and Walkman.

In November 1993, while playing his usual morning game of tennis, Morita fell down, and was diagnosed with cerebral hemorrhage. In the following years, he spent a long time in rehabilitation at his beachfront home near Diamond Head on the Hawaiian Island of Oahu, US. Partially paralysed and wheelchair-bound, his rehabilitation therapy involved speaking Japanese and English on alternate days. In December 1997 when Ibuka passed away, he was unable to come to attend his funeral, as he had been advised against travelling to Japan because of health reasons. Morita passed away on 3 October 1999. According to a Sony communiqué, he had been in a hospital in Tokyo since August the same year, and died of pneumonia.

His contribution to building the Sony brand remains unparalleled in corporate history and was hailed by many industry leaders. In a Harris poll of 1998, Sony was ranked No. 1, ahead of General Electric and Coca-Cola. *Time* magazine had described him as 'one of the 20 most influential geniuses of the twentieth century', making him the only non-American on the list.

Tributes and condolences poured in from different quarters on the announcement of his death. Mike Mansfield, former senator and the US Ambassador to the US, said, 'He was truly a statesman par excellence... Internationally, he did more for Japan in a business sense than anyone else in Japan.' Japan's prime minister

Keizō Obuchi, who was among about 400 people who visited his home following his death, was quoted by Kyodo News Service as saying 'Morita was a leading figure who played a pivotal role in developing Japan's post-war economy.' In the words of Sony President Nobuyuki Idei, 'It's not an exaggeration to say that he was the face of Japan.'

His contributions to his country and the industry in general were formally recognized by a number of different honours and awards that had been conferred on him. During his lifetime, Morita was honoured with the Golden Plate Award of the American Academy of Achievement in 1972; Albert Medal by UK's Royal Society of Arts in 1982—the first Japanese to receive it; Legion of Honour by the French government in 1984; First Class Order of the Sacred Treasure by the Emperor of Japan in 1993 and British Knighthood, KBE in 1993. In 1999, he was posthumously awarded the prestigious Japanese award, the Order of the Rising Sun. He was also vice chairman of the Japan Business Federation, and a member of the Japan-US Economic Relations Group, also called the 'Wise Men's Group'.

MEMORY BYTES—BIG AND SMALL, SWEET AND SOUR

In an over seven-decades long history, any company would go through a variety of ups and downs, strong and lean phases, and even interesting twists and turns. Numerous stories would be embedded in its folds, waiting to be told to the world. Stories that reveal how a small suggestion produced a major breakthrough, or a chance happening turned the tide of events in favour of the company—nuggets of information that make the story of a company spicy and lively.

Sony is no exception to this rule. Here are some glimpses of events that made their own contribution in Sony's long journey and helped shape its destiny.

A Journey—Rather a Mission!

Once Morita had made up his mind about joining Ibuka's company, the next step was seeking permission from his father, Kyusaemon the 14th (being the fourteenth generation in the business he was styled thus). His father presided over an old, established sake and soy sauce business which was in operation since 1665. Although according to the family tradition, it was expected of the eldest son to take over the business, having seen young Akio's inclinations towards a different side, his father was coming around to the fact that that was not to be. As a caring and sensible father, he would rather go along with the son's wishes rather than alienate him.

So, in April 1946, the would-be partners decided to take a journey to the Morita home to meet Akio's father. Given the sensitivity of the 'mission', Ibuka, for moral support, also managed to persuade his father-in-law Tamon Maeda to accompany them. It was an uncomfortable night journey from Tokyo to Kosugaya for the three of them, in an old rambling rail coach, with cold wind and soot blowing through the broken windows. On the other side, Morita's father had perhaps already decided to go along with the son's wishes. Not only did he give his blessings, he also agreed to make an investment in the new company. By some estimates, the Morita family's investment in Sony today is worth about $6 billion.

What's in a Name?

'That which we call a rose, by any other name would smell as sweet,' says Shakespeare's Juliet. But if you ask Sony, a name can make all the difference. And they've been proved right too.

When the company was formed in 1946, its abbreviation 'Totsuko', short for Tokyo Tsushin Kogyo Kabushiki Kaisha (Tokyo Telecommunications Engineering Corporation) resonated well with Japanese audiences. In fact, many companies with typically Japanese names like Toshiba, Hitachi, Mitsubishi, Toyota, etc. had been able to build strong brand recall value. But when Ibuka and Morita began to travel abroad, they felt the need to change the name of the company. They found that people in the US and Europe found it difficult to pronounce 'Totsuko.' They even pronounced Ibuka as, 'I-byu-ka'. Since they had a global vision and wanted their company to go international, they wanted a name that would go well with diverse consumers, would be easy to pronounce and have a strong recall value.

First, they thought of an abbreviation of three–four letters. There were already examples of many three-letter brands like RCA, NBS, CBS, NHK, etc. and so they narrowed it down to TTK that sounded quite 'corporate.' Later, however, they realized that it sounded quite similar to TKK, the nomenclature that had been adopted by the Japanese railway company, Tokyo Kyuko. Having tried many permutations and combinations, the company finally decided on 'Sony', which was easy to pronounce and subtly referred to their operation. It was a combination of 'sonus' (the Latin origin for 'sound' and 'sonic') and 'Sonny' (American nickname for young boys who make up with energy what they lack in experience). To begin with, the 'Sony' name was used for the company's products, such as Sony Tape, Sony Tape recorder, etc. with 'Totsuko' used for the company. In 1958, 'Sony' was formally adopted as the corporate name.

Frank Sinatra's Fascination

In late April 1962, when Frank Sinatra paid a visit to Sony, he was quite taken with the five-inch TV5-303 — so much so that he wanted to take one along with him to the US. Since it had not yet been launched in the US and the channels in Japan were different from those of America, Morita promised to deliver one to Sinatra when the TV was readjusted to American specifications. The TV went on sale in the US six months later. Morita kept his word, and he himself went to deliver the TV to Sinatra at Paramount Pictures, where he was shooting for a film.

A Japanese Fan to the Rescue

In 1982, Sony along with Philips had developed an audio CD which would be a replacement of the conventional vinyl LP. There was a need to build awareness about the new product, and demonstrations of the CD were held in different parts of the world. As both the hardware and the CD were in the prototype stage, there was a fear of things going haywire. So, during a press conference in New York while demonstrating their new product to the audience, an engineer, somewhere in the background, was desperately trying to prevent the system from overheating by cooling it off with a Japanese paper fan!

Speeding Ticket for Testing TV

During the development of their five-inch TV for cars, the Sony engineers wished to test the performance of the prototype in a car at high speeds. They wanted to see how it would withstand vibrations, the effect of the intercepting radio waves on its performance, besides that of the noise generated by the car while in motion. During some of these secret test drives on a 600-km stretch of expressway, the team had had some interesting experiences. Curious truck drivers would try to peer into the car to see if there was anything suspicious going on. And on one occasion, the car was stopped by the police for speeding, and they even had a good first look at the yet-to-be marketed five-inch car TV.

'Please Keep This a Secret, Your Majesty!'

In the beginning of the 1960s, Sony's reputation as an innovator and a pioneer in electronic items had begun to spread far and wide in the country. In 1962, the Emperor and Empress of Japan decided to visit the Sony plant in Tokyo to see for themselves the progress being made by the company. Acting as guides, Ibuka and Morita showed the imperial majesties the production line and the products being developed. At the climax of the tour, the royal couple was shown the prototype of the micro-five-inch car TV. Since it was yet to be announced, they asked the Emperor and Empress to keep it confidential. Somehow the news leaked and many major newspapers went to town with the scoop, with news lines such as: 'Emperor hushed up!' 'Sony's pocket-sized television, produced under top-secret conditions...Their Imperial majesties were asked to keep confidentiality.'

Going to Work in Gumboots

After having signed the licence for transistors with Western Electric, US, the next step for Totsuko (Sony) was to have its own materials plant in Japan. Having considered different options, they finally settled on Sendai, the capital of Miyagi Prefecture (district), 363 km from Tokyo. Given the post-war conditions and Sony's requirements, the location they got to select was a farmland amidst paddy fields, many of which would be flooded from time to time. Thus, one of the first tasks of the management after the plant opened in May 1954 was to acquire 27 pairs of rubber boots for the first batch of personnel.

A Million-dollar Robbery or Publicity!

Well, for Sony, it was about a $100,000 loss, but the publicity was surely worth millions!

In the late 1950s, Sony's transistor-radio model TR-63 had become extremely popular—to the extent that it had caught the imagination of burglars too. On a January morning in 1958, Sony executive Hiroshi Tada, who was in New York to prepare for the opening of a Sony office, came to know that 4,000 Sony transistors worth $100,000 had been stolen from their distributor Delmonico's warehouse in Long Island. Interestingly, the burglars, who had boldly driven up in a truck, didn't touch the products of other manufacturers that had also been kept there. The next morning, *The New York Times* carried a bold headline, '4000 Japanese Transistor Radios Stolen from Delmonico's Warehouse.'

Some loss, but it was great publicity for Sony, which was trying to make its presence felt in the US.

Saved by IBM

In the mid-1960s, as Sony had collaborated with IBM in magnetic tape technology and signed technology-sharing agreement, the two companies had come to enjoy certain understanding and goodwill between them. Around 1966, Sony began to experience serious financial stress, first on account of cost overruns due to its Chromatron project, and second because of the US equalizing tax (of 16.5 per cent) that the country had begun to levy on the foreign capital leaving the US, which had brought the Japanese economy under stress.

Under these circumstances, Sony decided to seek IBM's help to bail them out of the situation — and the man delegated with this responsibility was Noboru Yoshii, a former banker with Mitsui Bank, who had joined Sony in 1961. Interestingly, he also had had a personal stake in the negotiations going well, as he owned 20,000 Sony shares, which had depreciated considerably on account of the general slump. Fortunately for Sony and himself, the talks with IBM were fruitful and the company decided to make an appreciable investment in Sony. This news came, not only as a huge relief to Sony, but also cheered the Japanese stock market. Yoshii's investment more than doubled and he was out of the financial straits.

SONY—TODAY AND TOMORROW

Today when you watch your favourite serial on TV or record a family function on a video camera, listen to the latest hit by Alicia Keys or play a pulse-racing game on PlayStation, you know you're with Sony. Far, far away from the scenic environs of Nikko, where Ibuka was born or Sony's first bleak, window-less radio repair shop in a bombed-out department store in Nihonbashi, Tokyo. Sony has indeed come a long way from its early days in 1946, to a realm much wider and larger, as dreamt of by its founders.

Sony is now a global entity with presence in all the seven continents. It had an annual revenue of $76.938 billion as of 2020 financial year, and is ranked 122 in Fortune's Global 500 list. In its history of over 70 years, it has traversed a long journey, marked by a variety of challenges and successes, and has maintained a steady growth.

However, it was only in the beginning of the new millennium that it had begun to experience a slowdown with revenues stagnating, or even falling with some losses, as we've discussed in 'Life after Founders'. Things have surely begun to look up since then. 'In the fiscal year ended March 31 2019, we achieved record profits for the second consecutive year, as the initiatives we have been implementing over the last few years bore fruit,' noticed with some satisfaction Kenichiro Yoshida in the Corporate Report 2019.[15] As mentioned earlier, Yoshida along with his mentor Kazuo Hirai, had been able to turn the tide in their favour by taking some very aggressive steps and strategic decisions. As a result, in the recent years, Sony's share has continued to rise, after having touched a historic low of $14.49 in 2012 and now going up to $106.93 as of 26 February 2021. Any entity, individual or corporate, continues to go through certain course-correction depending upon the circumstances. And Sony was fortunate to have some very capable people to address its problems.

Following strategic restructuring over the years, the company is now set on a definite path with a clear agenda. It is a mix of some conventional businesses like consumer electronics, entertainment and financial services, and state-of-the-art digital technology-driven products like advanced semiconductors, interactive games, robotics and AI. As far as the conventional businesses are concerned, any company executive would agree that given some smart and judicious management, they can be taken care of, and would continue to yield desired results. A clear example in this context is that of the Sony TV. While market analysts were earlier advising the company to move out of the electronics business, according to 2021 reports, Sony TV (with its flagship Bravia brand) is at the third position in ratings, after the two Korean brands, LG and Samsung. 'Our progress in the fiscal year ended March 31, 2019 can be measured by the growth of PSN (PlayStation Network), which has become one of the world's leading network services,' noted Yoshida in Sony's Corporate Report 2019.[16] Beginning just as one of the product-activities in the mid-1990s for the company, Sony's PlayStation has come to hold the top position in the console game market, and the PlayStation 4 is expected to reach an all-time high of 100 million units sold by the end of fiscal year 31 March 2020.

As a segment, Games and Network Services (G&NS) has posted the largest sales and profit ever recorded by a single segment of Sony, in which the PlayStation had contributed 60 per cent of revenue. Broadly speaking, currently while other segments like music, pictures, semiconductors, home entertainment, financial services, etc. each contributed in the range of 10–15 per cent to the total revenue for the company, G&NS has been contributing upwards of 20 per cent. Given these trends, not only to Sony, but to the industry in general, it's becoming increasingly clear that in the coming time, a variety of products and businesses would be driven by futuristic digital technologies.

Semiconductor Technology Giving Sony an Edge

It's important to note here that from the early days when the transistor was invented at Bell Labs, semiconductor technology too has come a long way. The critical change and advancement in this respect took place in 1959 when the MOSFET (metal-oxide-semiconductor-field-effect transistor), or MOS, was invented by Mohamed M. Atalla and Dawon Kahng at Bell Labs, US and was patented the following year. Since then, it has remained the 'essential' semiconductor or the basic building block of all advanced electronic devices.

At the time of its development, the inventors demonstrated two types of fabrication processes: 'n' type and 'p' type. Later, in 1963, Chih-Tang Sah and Frank Wanlass, working at Fairchild Semiconductor, went a step further and adapted and combined the two processes to produce a semiconductor that came to be known as complimentary MOS (CMOS). Given its advantages, from 1980 onwards, it came to be the standard device for producing advanced VLSIs (very large-scale integration) chips. It has since become the industry standard for most of the sophisticated electronic devices, and it is estimated that as of 2011, the process was used for fabrication of VLSI chips in 99 per cent cases. In the words of Yoshida, 'CMOS image sensors are not only indispensable in image capturing and content creation, they are also key devices for the future in areas such as the Internet of Things (IoT), AI and autonomous driving.'

From Sony's point of view, general growth in digital arena in the recent times has been a favourable development. It is evident that while regular businesses are less of a concern, the real challenge—and power and glory—however lies in taking the road less travelled, in specialized areas that remain the preserve of an exclusive few. Sony had experienced this in the 1950s while developing the tape recorder and later transistor technology. As a result, besides capturing some lucrative markets, it was also able to build certain expertise and know-how in the semiconductor technology earlier on in the day. At a time when the semiconductors are virtually driving the universe, this expertise has begun to pay the company handsome dividends. Sony's growing expertise in the semiconductor technology has begun to enhance its business prospects at different levels in diverse areas.

First, being a leading semiconductor manufacturer, it is also a major supplier of the most advanced semiconductors to a large number of companies, for their next-generation products. In his foreword to the 2019 Corporate Report, Yoshida had observed that one of the reasons for their increased profits was because of 'the CMOS image sensors which replaced CCDs as the mainstay product of our semiconductors business in 2004'.[17] In 2019, the company retained its No. 1 position in 'imaging applications for CMOS image sensors by delivering a stable supply to the smartphone market, which is evolving not only toward higher resolution, but also toward multi-camera lenses and larger sized sensors'. Sony's sensor devices were also adopted by a large automotive manufacturer, besides its technologically-superior indirect Time of Flight (iToF) sensors by some smartphone manufacturers. In future, the company plans to embed AI into its CMOS image sensors and realize Edge AI, or 'intelligence at the edge'.

Given the general trend, Sony has ambitious future plans to make aggressive forays in the digital space. On 20 November 2019, it announced the establishment of Sony AI, with offices at strategic locations around the globe. With an aim to take research to the next level in 'imaging and sensing solutions, robotics and entertainment (Games, Music and Movies)', it seeks to 'fill the world with emotion, through power of creativity and technology'.[18] And on 19 August 2019, Sony announced its decision to acquire Insomniac Games Inc., which has been a long-time partner of Sony, and also the developer of Sony PlayStation's top-selling Marvel's Spider-Man and hugely popular PlayStation's Ratchet and Clank franchise. With Sony's interactive games on an upward trajectory, the company has been on a big buying spree of late, with Insomniac Games Inc. being the fourteenth studio to join the Sony Interactive entertainment's family since its inception.

In this era of specialization, it makes better business sense to have a strategic tie-up rather than grow oneself in isolation. In May 2019, Sony and Microsoft signed a Memorandum of Understanding (MoU) to partner on 'new innovations to enhance customer experience in their direct-to-consumer entertainment platforms and AI solutions'.[19]

We must note here that both Sony and Microsoft are leaders in computer games, with their flagship products PlayStation and Xbox closely competing with each other. Under this arrangement, the companies decided to explore joint-development of future Cloud solutions in Microsoft's Azure to support their respective game and content-streaming services. Additionally, Sony being a leader in semiconductor technology, the companies also decided to collaborate in developing new intelligent image sensor solutions to provide enhanced capabilities for enterprise customers. Again, in May 2020, the two companies decided to partner for developing smart camera solutions for enterprise customers. Such cameras would be capable of extracting useful information out of images in smart cameras and other devices.

Digital technology-driven products are the cash cows for the company for now and the future. It doesn't mean however that conventional businesses like electronics, films, music, etc. would be ignored. To boost business prospects in these areas, Sony has been taking a variety of proactive measures in recent years—which include acquisitions, promotional events and innovative new initiatives.

In September 2017, Sony reached an agreement with Lino Manfrotto & Co. for production and marketing of a broad range of cameras (digital and video) and accessories for professionals, travelers' use, etc. The Italian camera manufacturing company, established in 1972, has developed an expertise in producing a variety of top-of-the-line cameras and accessories, many of which have become the industry standard.

In August 2016, Sony acquired TEN Sports from ZEE Entertainment Enterprises Ltd, for $385 million. 'I welcome TEN Sports to the Sony family,' said N.P. Singh, CEO, Sony Pictures Television Networks India. 'The acquisition of TEN Sports Network will strengthen SPN's offering for viewers of cricket, football and fight sports, complementing our existing portfolio of international and domestic sporting properties.'[20] In July 2017, the company announced acquisition of the majority stake in Funimation, a Japanese anime distributor and the No.1 English-language anime content provider in North America. With a catalog that includes popular titles like Dragon Ball Z, Cowboy Bebop, One Piece, My Hero Academia and others, it remains a leader in its field.

In the music arena, Sony Music UK announced in August 2016, the acquisition of Ministry of Sound Recordings Ltd, UK, which has been one of the most successful dance-music labels, with a cumulative sale in the excess of 70 million, showcasing the talents of Jodie Abacus, Louise Berry, Moss Kena, Eric Prydz, Example and others.

Further, 'Lost in Music' and '360 Reality Audio' have been some of the most innovative musical concepts created by the company in the recent times. 'Lost in Music' is a periodical event whose third installment took place in November 2018 in New York. Described as an 'immersive pop-up space in New York City bringing together the very best of Sony technology and Sony Music artists', the initiative seeks to bring the viewers an enhanced musical experience through 'a weekly

YouTube show, exclusive and intimate performances by various artists, along with debut of an interactive song creation experience and a space to experience multi-dimensional audio technology'.

And then, '360 Reality Audio', announced in October 2019, is an altogether new experience for any music lover, with streaming services from different sources. It promises to be 'an immersive audio experience utilizing spatial audio technology'. The listeners would be able to access approximately 1,000 songs by artists such as Mark Ronson and Pharrell Williams through streaming services Amazon Music HD, Deezer, nugs.net and TIDAL. For the listener, the experience would be of sound coming from different directions, giving the feel of a live musical performance.

With programmes such as these and other initiatives, the company has been going ahead full-steam in pursuit of its goals. Given the current market trends and Sony's inherent strengths, the company is set to charter a brave new course to cross many an important milestone in future.

EPILOGUE

Innovation is the key. An electric bulb lights up your life and you marvel at the genius of the inventor. A motor car changes the way you live, and you thank your stars for being born in the modern times. A cell phone instantly connects you to a loved one and you begin to feel happy and relaxed. Smart ideas and inventions have always continued to drive people and their dreams.

Ibuka, himself a dreamer, was well aware of this fact. So, when the world was making radios, he thought of the tape recorder. When even the licensees didn't give transistors a shot beyond being used in a hearing device, he made a truly commercially successful transistor radio with it. When his own colleagues at Sony were apprehensive about the success of a taping device that didn't record, he turned the Walkman into an all-time market phenomenon. Out-of-the-box thinking and going the extra mile have been the pathways to innovation, and also the secret of Sony's success.

Sony's long and eventful life story no doubt then leaves us with a loud and clear message: focus on people's needs, help them fulfill their dreams and you'll go far in life.

REFERENCES

1. 'Japan-Religious Affiliation 2017.' *Statista*, www.statista. com/statistics/237609/religions-in-japan/. Accessed on 20 January 2021. Accessed on 20 January 2021

2. 'The Founding Prospectus.' *SONY*, www.sony.net/ SonyInfo/CorporateInfo/History/prospectus.html. Accessed on 20 January 2021.

3. Nathan, John. *Sony: The Private Life*. HarperCollins Business, 2001.

4. Before WWII, the yen traded roughly at 3.6 to a dollar. After the end of the war with the occupation forces taking over, an exchange rate of 15 to one dollar was fixed. As the economy slipped, different rates of exchange came into force: 50 to one in 1946; 270 to one in 1948; and finally, 360 to one dollar in 1949. Subsequently, it kept on fluctuating, and stands at 104.95 as of 13 February 2021.

5. Metals like iron, copper, aluminium, etc. are good conductors of electricity, while materials like wood and rubber are insulators or bad conductors. To produce

advanced and sophisticated electrical and electronic products, there was a need for some intermediate substances that would allow greater manipulation and regulation of current through a device. Vacuum tubes served this purpose to an extent, but had their limitations. Research and experimentation over a long period of time finally yielded silicon, germanium and gallium arsenide as the right base materials to build semiconductors on. Given their unique properties, it became possible to produce semiconductors that would allow passing of current more easily in one direction than the other; permit variable resistance to current within a device; and allow for variable degrees of sensitivity to heat and light by a component. These features facilitated amplification, switching and energy conservation within a product. A common example of a semiconductor is a 'diode' that allows the flow of current only in one direction.

6. Tabuchi, Hiroko. 'How the Tech Parade Passed Sony By.' *The New York Times*, 14 April 2012, www.nytimes.com/2012/04/15/technology/how-sony-fell-behind-in-the-tech-parade.html. Accessed on 20 January 2021.
7. Tabuchi, Hiroko. 'Sony's Bread and Butter? It's Not Electronics.' *The New York Times*, 28 May 2013, www.nytimes.com/2013/05/28/business/global/sonys-bread-and-butter-its-not-electronics.html. Accessed on 20 January 2021.

8. Nathan, John. *Sony: The Private Life*. HarperCollins Business, 2001.

9. Ibid.

10. 'Press Release: Masaru Ibuka 1908–1997.' *SONY*, www.sony.net/SonyInfo/News/Press_Archive/199801/ibuka-e.html. Accessed on 20 January 2021.

11. Nathan, John. *Sony: The Private Life*. HarperCollins Business, 2001.

12. Pollack, Andrew. 'Akio Morita, Co-Founder of Sony and Japanese Business Leader, Dies at 78.' *The New York Times*, 4 October 1999, www.nytimes.com/1999/10/04/business/akio-morita-co-founder-of-sony-and-japanese-business-leader-dies-at-78.html. Accessed on 20 January 2021.

13. Ishihara, S. Shintaro. *The Japan That Can Say No*. Translated by F. Baldwin, Simon & Schuster, 1991.

14. Pollack, Andrew. 'Akio Morita, Co-Founder of Sony and Japanese Business Leader, Dies at 78.' *The New York Times*, 4 October 1999, www.nytimes.com/1999/10/04/business/akio-morita-co-founder-of-sony-and-japanese-business-leader-dies-at-78.html. Accessed on 20 January 2021.

15. 'Corporate Report.' *SONY*, www.sony.net/SonyInfo/IR/library/corporatereport/. Accessed on 20 January 2021.

16. Ibid.

17. Ibid.

18. 'Sony Announces the Establishment of Sony AI with

the Mission to Unleash Human Creativity.' *Sony Global*, www.sony.net/SonyInfo/News/Press/201911/19-118E/. Accessed on 20 January 2021.

19. 'Sony and Microsoft to Explore Strategic Partnership Companies to Collaborate on New Cloud-Based Solutions for Gaming Experiences and AI Solutions.' *Sony Global*, www.sony.net/SonyInfo/News/Press/201905/19-0517E/. Accessed on 20 January 2021.

20. 'Sony Pictures to Acquire Ten Sports from Zee.' *Sony Pictures Entertainment*, www.sonypictures.com/corp/press_releases/2016/08_16/083116_tensports.html. Accessed on 20 January 2021.

BIBLIOGRAPHY

'After 5-Year Slump, Sony Back in Black in First Half.' *Nikkei Asia*, 29 October 2015, asia.nikkei.com/NAR/Articles/After-5-year-slump-Sony-back-in-black-in-first-half. Accessed on 12 January 2021.

'Akio Morita.' *Encyclopedia.com*, www.encyclopedia.com/people/social-sciences-and-law/business-leaders/akio-morita. Accessed on 8 January 2021.

'Financial Information.' *Sony Financial Holdings*, www.sonyfh.co.jp/en/financial_info/. Accessed on 28 December 2020.

'Global Notebook PC Shipments 2019.' *Statista*, www.statista.com/statistics/234752/global-notebook-pc-shipments-by-brand/. Accessed on 8 January 2021.

'History of Japan.' *Japanese History*, www.japan-guide.com/e/e641.html. Accessed on 27 October 2020.

'History of Semiconductors.' *Hitachi High-Tech GLOBAL*, www.hitachi-hightech.com/global/products/device/semiconductor/history.html. Accessed on 24 December 2020.

'Ibuka Masaru.' *Encyclopædia Britannica*, www.britannica. com/biography/Ibuka-Masaru. Accessed on 20 December 2020.

'It All Began with a Failed Rice Cooker.' *GSM* Arena, www.gsmarena.com/it_all_began_with_a_failed_rice_ cooker__a_glimpse_at_sonys_history-blog-13661.php. Accessed on 22 November 2020.

'Kenichiro Yoshida.' *The Japan Times*, 23 May 2019, www. japantimes.co.jp/tag/kenichiro-yoshida/. Accessed on 18 January 2021.

'Kenichiro Yoshida.' *Variety*, 23 December 2020, variety.com/ exec/kenichiro-yoshida/. Accessed on 8 January 2021.

'Masaru Ibuka.' *Success Story*, successstory.com/people/ masaru-ibuka. Accessed on 9 January 2021.

'Meet Sony's New CEO Kenichiro Yoshida, the Enforcer of Its Turnaround.' *Fortune*, 2 February 2018, fortune. com/2018/02/02/sony-ceo-kaz-hirai-kenichiro-yoshida/. Accessed on 4 January 2021.

'Milestones: 1945–1952.' *U.S. Department of State*, history.state. gov/milestones/1945-1952/japan-reconstruction. Accessed on 7 January 2021.

'Morita Akio.' *Encyclopædia Britannica*, www.britannica.com/ biography/Morita-Akio. Accessed on 2 January 2021.

'PlayStation Inventor Starts New Career Making Robots for No Pay.' Livdose, livdose.com/news/technology/ playstation-inventor-starts-new-career-making-robots-for-no-pay/. Accessed on 21 January 2021.

'Shadow Masks and Aperture Grilles.' *Encyclopædia Britannica*, www.britannica.com/technology/television-technology/ Shadow-masks-and-aperture-grilles. Accessed on 10 January 2021.

'Sony Announces the Establishment of Sony AI with the Mission to Unleash Human Creativity.' *Sony Globa*, www.sony.net/SonyInfo/News/Press/201911/19-118E/. Accessed on 2 January 2021.

'Sony Comes Back from the Brink, and It's Not All Thanks to Spider-Man.' *The Guardian*, 4 November 2017, www. theguardian.com/technology/2017/nov/04/sony-record-profits-spider-man-playstation-crown. Accessed on 10 December 2020.

'Sony Entertainment News and Updates from The Economic Times - Page 2.' *The Economic Times,* economictimes. indiatimes.com/topic/Sony-Entertainment/news/2/2. Accessed on 22 January 2021.

'Sony Global Press Release: Masaru Ibuka 1908–1997.' *SONY,* www.sony.net/SonyInfo/News/Press_Archive/199801/ ibuka-e.html. Accessed on 28 December 2020.

'Sony Global—Annual Report.' *SONY,* www.sony.net/ SonyInfo/IR/library/ar/Archive.html. Accessed on 29 December 2020.

'Sony Global—Corporate Report.' *SONY,* www.sony.net/ SonyInfo/IR/library/corporatereport/. Accessed on 2 January 2021.

'Sony Global—History.' *SONY,* www.sony.net/SonyInfo/

CorporateInfo/History/. Accessed on 24 November 2020.

'Sony Global—News Releases.' *SONY*, www.sony.net/ SonyInfo/News/Press/. Accessed on 28 December 2020.

'Sony Revenue 2007–2019.' *Statista*, www.statista.com/ statistics/279269/total-revenue-of-sony-since-2008/. Accessed on 29 December 2020.

'Sony Sales by Business Segments 2012–2019.' *Statista*, www. statista.com/statistics/297533/sony-sales-worldwide-by-business-segment/. Accessed on 26 November 2020.

'Sony to Sell off Vaio Laptop Division in Effort to Stem Huge Losses.' *The Guardian*, 6 February 2014, www.theguardian. com/technology/2014/feb/06/sony-vaio-laptop-losses-bravia-tv. Accessed on 29 December 2020.

'Sony, Microsoft Consoles Struggle with Thin Launch-Day Stock.' Yahoo! Finance, ca.finance.yahoo.com/news/sony-microsoft-consoles-struggle-thin-095431992.html. Accessed on 23 January 2021.

'Sony—47 Year Stock Price History: SNE.' *Macrotrends*, www. macrotrends.net/stocks/charts/SNE/sony/stock-price-history. Accessed on 18 December 2020.

'Sony's Exit from the PC Market Will Not Be the Last.' *The Guardian*, 6 February 2014, www.theguardian.com/ technology/2014/feb/06/sony-vaio-exit-pc-market-analysis. Accessed on 18 December 2020.

'The Humanities.' *Encyclopædia Britannica*, www.britannica. com/topic/history-of-Europe/The-humanities. Accessed on 22 November 2020.

'The Principle of Semiconductor.' *Nanotec Museum*, www. tel.com/museum/exhibition/principle/. Accessed on 18 December 2020.

'The Top 10 Movie Production Companies of All Time - ReelRundown - Entertainment.' ReelRundown, 6 July 2014, reelrundown.com/film-industry/Top-10-Movie-Production-Companies. Accessed on 11 January 2021.

'What Was the Japanese Economic Miracle?' *WorldAtlas*, 22 August 2019, www.worldatlas.com/articles/what-was-the-japanese-economic-miracle.html. Accessed on 7 January 2021.

'Why Sony's Trinitron Tubes Were the Best.' *Hackaday*, 3 January 2018, hackaday.com/2018/01/03/why-sonys-trinitron-tubes-were-the-best/. Accessed on 7 January 2021.

'World History.' *Encyclopædia Britannica*, www.britannica. com/browse/World-History. Accessed on 29 October 2020.

'World War I.' *History.com*, 29 October 2009, www.history. com/topics/world-war-i/world-war-i-history. Accessed on 1 November 2020.

Cartwright, Mark. 'Ancient Japan.' *Ancient History Encyclopedia*, 22 February 2021, www.ancient.eu/Ancient_Japan/. Accessed on 26 October 2020.

Farquhar, Dave. 'Why VHS Beat Betamax.' *The Silicon Underground*, 29 March 2019, dfarq.homeip.net/why-vhs-beat-betamax/. Accessed on 8 January 2021.

Fasol, Gerhard. 'Masaru Ibuka 1908–97.' *Nature News*, www.nature.com/articles/36007?error=cookies_not_

supported&code=   1125d105-c3bc-4fe8-8ee0-fe58cffdcdc3. Accessed on 8 January 2021.

Hays, Jeffrey. 'HISTORY OF EDUCATION IN JAPAN.' *Facts and Details*, factsanddetails.com/japan/cat23/sub150/ entry-2794.html. Accessed on 10 January 2021.

Knight, Will. 'Sony Envisions an AI-Fueled World, From Kitchen Bots to Games.' *Wired, Conde Nast*, www.wired. com/story/sony-envisions-ai-fueled-world-kitchen-bots-games/. Accessed on 8 January 2021.

Murphy, Mike. 'Sony Doesn't Want to Compete on Price, so It's Going Back to Its Premium Roots.' *Quartz*, qz.com/1190630/ sony-doesnt-want-to-compete-on-price-so-its-going-back-to-its-premium-roots/. Accessed on 22 December 2020.

Nathan, John. *Sony: The Private Life*. HarperCollins Business, 2001.

Pollack, Andrew. 'Akio Morita, Co-Founder of Sony and Japanese Business Leader, Dies at 78.' *The New York Times*, 4 October 1999, www.nytimes.com/1999/10/04/business/ akio-morita-co-founder-of-sony-and-japanese-business-leader-dies-at-78.html. Accessed on 8 January 2021.

Tabuchi, Hiroko. 'Sony's Bread and Butter? It's Not Electronics.' *The New York Times*, www.nytimes.com/2013/05/28/ business/global/sonys-bread-and-butter-its-not-electronics. html. Accessed on 29 December 2020.